There is an Occupation...

Miriam M. Mahy

D0166676

Dedicated to my husband Bill
without whose help this book
would not have been written.

THERE IS AN OCCUPATION

I was born in 1914 to Alfred Mahy and Mary Ann (née Nicolle). My sister followed in 1917 and my mother died in the terrible 'flu epidemic of 1918.

Three years later my father married Eunice le Masurier from Jersey and there were two children of that marriage, Hazel and Lucille. We lived at 'Rockdale', La Turquie, Vale.

Wilson Mahy (Bill) and I were married in 1935 and lived at the Old Marais until 1945. Bill's mother and father, Henri and Eliza (née Hubert) lived at the Hougue Père. There were six children, Henry, Phyllis, Wilson, Eileen, Charlotte and John.

We were married eleven years before our first daughter, Jane, was born in 1946, then followed by her two sisters, Carol and Sarah. Our daughters are married, respectively, to Jeremy Smithies, Roland Guille and Stuart Crisp.

We have seven grand children: Carol-Anne Stapley, Nicholas Rowe, Emma Curtis, Elizabeth Ruddy, Roland Guille, William Crisp and Jack Crisp. There are eight great grandchildren: Joanna and Tom Stapley, Chloe and Peter Curtis, James, Edward and Harry Ruddy and Eva Guille.

Miriam M. Mahy

First published 1992
Reprints 1993, 2007

Printed in Great Britain by
Creeds the Printers, Broadoak, Bridport, Dorset DT6 5NL.

ISBN 0 9519767 0 2

CONTENTS

The author and her husband taken just before the war.

Chapter 1

RUMOUR OF INVASION

It all began that Sunday morning, September 3rd 1939 at 11 a.m. when we stood by the wireless set in the living room and heard Neville Chamberlain's precise voice saying, "England is at war with Germany". We expected everything to change but life went on very much as before. That first year has often been called 'The Phoney War'. We were given instructions and issued with gas masks. We sang patriotic songs with gusto, 'There'll always be an England' and very popular were 'We'll hang out the washing on the Siegfried Line' and Gracie Fields' 'Wish me luck as you wave me goodbye'. We still grew our tomatoes, attended our meetings and social gatherings. We bought a case of tea, half a hundredweight of sugar and two or three dozen tins of fruit.

In the spring of 1940 the news was disquieting. The Allies were being pushed back, and over the wireless, Hitler's harsh ranting voice and the roars of applause from his followers sent a chill of apprehension down our spines.

As the summer progressed, refugees from France were seen in the island and everyone was so sorry that they had been driven from their homes but glad that they had found refuge in Guernsey. We did not, or would not, see our own dangerous position, the islands cradled in the arm of France and Hitler's armies rapidly approaching the coast.

June appeared with blue skies and brilliant sunshine, a glorious summer had arrived. The day dawned when we could hear the guns roaring in France and see a blanket of smoke on the horizon.

On one beautiful day, the 19th June, many mothers were enjoying the sunshine on the beach with their small children when messengers came running amongst them with the dreaded message, "There's going to be an occupation, women and children are to be evacuated, meet for instructions at the parish schools."

In a few minutes the beaches were empty, rumour and counter-rumour spread like wildfire, but one fact remained, the Germans were coming and England was sending boats to collect evacuees. People had to meet at the schools for information and instructions.

The owner of a shoe shop on the Bridge was throwing footwear on the street for anyone to pick up so that the Germans would not have it. Panic reigned. Bill and I rushed to town to buy two travelling trunks for evacuation. People gathered in little groups around their front gates. Should they go? Should they stay? So many dogs were taken to the vets to be put down that they could not cope, they gave people the lethal tablets to give to their own pets.

Our dog, Chum, followed us everywhere with a hanging tail and refused to eat his food. He was definitely aware that something was very wrong.

My two great-aunts, Rachel Le Poidevin and Mary Bougourd, lived in their cottage at Cocagne. They were both over 80 years and when I visited them during the turmoil of the evacuation, they were busily cleaning their house and a line of snowy washing hung on the clothes line.

"Tchique donc qué vou-s-êtes à faire?" I asked what she was doing in patois because Aunt Mary did not speak English. "You know that the latest news is that everyone must go to England."

Aunt Rachel replied, "If we have to go away we want to leave everything clean and in order and when the Germans come in they will see that clean and decent people lived here."

On the other hand, some people left with the breakfast table uncleared and unmade beds upstairs, with the attitude, "Let the enemy clear up the mess."

Cyril Bird rode across the Bridge on his bike calling, "The war is almost over, the Russians are joining the Allies and Hitler is being held."

Cyril had this bright idea to calm the people and stop panic. One man who heard the glad tidings rushed home to tell his wife and, for the first time since the evacuation was mentioned, he ate a hearty meal then relaxed to hear the one o'clock news. Alas Alvar Liddel did not mention the Russians, his news was of retreating armies, of air and shipping losses, the man went outside and was sick!

It was a heartbreaking time. Terrible decisions had to be made. Shall we send our children with the school party or will mother go with them leaving husband behind? What about the babies and toddlers? Dare we take the responsibility of keeping the children in Guernsey with the threat of enemy occupation hanging over us? The whole of Thursday was spent going to and fro to the schools or to the harbour with packed suitcases; the promised evacuation boats had not yet arrived.

On Wednesday evening my brother-in-law, among other anxious parents, attended the meeting held at the Vale Parish School. An official was going to explain the evacuation procedure. The first boat would leave the following morning with women and small children.

My brother-in-law, his wife and family were at school at 10 a.m. The expected boat had not yet arrived at the harbour. It was oppressively hot and they, in company with other families, waited and waited for further instructions. When lunchtime arrived and there was still no news from the harbour, the families returned home for a meal. They were told to return at 2 p.m. As my brother-in-law, his wife and two children aged five and two, walked down the 'Croix du Bois' hill they met Mrs. Louise Corbet, red faced and panting.

"Don't worry, the Russians have entered the war, the danger is over, it won't last long now."

She then explained to the family that she also had planned to evacuate and had given instructions to a man to go and wring the necks of the fowls in her back garden but, having heard the encouraging news, she was now hurrying home hoping to be in time to stop him.

When my brother-in-law switched on the one o'clock news, he knew that it was all rumour and that nothing had changed. The family walked sadly back to school. During the afternoon two year old Robert had managed to get so black in the dusty playground that his mother took him to his aunt, who lived nearby, for a bath.

The day passed and the weary crowd was told to return the next morning when the first ship was due to arrive.

The first boats carrying women and children left on Friday morning, the 21st June. My sister-in-law left at 11 a.m. with her two little ones. Her husband was carrying Robert and a suitcase and he tried to carry him along the gangplank on to the boat to help his wife settle in. This was not permitted. It was feared that men would try to smuggle themselves on to the boats which were strictly for women and children. My brother-in-law was forced to watch his wife struggle on to the boat with the two infants and their luggage. They had previously made a pact that, as Big Ben sounded the first stroke before the 9 o'clock news, they would think of each other. Two or three weeks at the most was what they had in mind, not five years.

One man insisted that his wife should seek safety in England, but after she had gone he was so miserable he left on the first available boat taking men.

In the meanwhile, after being in England a couple of days, the wife thought, "What am I doing here? I'm going back to my home and Fred, come what may." She managed to get on the last boat to Guernsey and when the Germans landed the following day she was here and her husband was in England.

Because the evacuation boats did not arrive promptly when expected, the island was fraught with anxiety and indecision. The order was that women with infants and schools with helpers and staff would evacuate first, then men of military age, and afterwards, if there were enough boats, anyone could leave.

The final assembly for the Vale School was for 11 p.m. My parents, Alfred and Eunice Mahy, had been backwards and forwards with Lucille, their nine year old child, clutching her small suitcase, her big brown eyes large and puzzled. At 10 p.m. my parents entered Lucille's bedroom to awaken her for the long trip to England.

The author, Miriam, (back left) with 3 sisters, Lucille (back right) Hazel and Evelyn (front left and right).

They looked at their peaceful, sleeping child and then looked at each other.

"What are we doing?" my father asked. "We're preparing to send this little one in the middle of the night to an unknown destination with a crowd of children and a few teachers and helpers. She's never left home or been parted from her family. If we send her, we should go as well. We've decided to stay in Guernsey, and come what may, families should stay together and take what comes together." The evacuation boat left at midnight without Lucille, and without several other children whose parents had had time to think the situation over and had come to the same conclusion as my father. Had the boat left at the appointed time, these children would have gone.

The boats left with their cargoes of confused and frightened humanity and husbands promised their weeping wives that they would follow on the first available boat.

The author, Miriam, (on right) with her sister Evelyn, just before the war in 1939.

Chapter 2

THE HEARTBREAK OF SEPARATION

After the main evacuation boats had gone, Bill's parents at the Hougue Père were bewildered and worried. Fourteen year old John was thrilled by the situation and he shouted a last excited goodbye and left to join his comrades of the Boys' Intermediate School.

"Goodbye mum, I'll be shaving when I come back," he called. How right he was.

Bill's sisters, Phyllis and Charlotte who lived at home, were very unsettled and uneasy. Many of their friends had gone and they tried in vain to persuade their parents to evacuate.

One morning 18 year old Charlotte went to her brother Henry's vinery where he was picking tomatoes.

"I'd like to go away," she said, "I'm afraid that the Germans may come and there's nothing to keep me here except mum and pop and they've still got you, Phyl, Bill and Eileen. Bob, my boyfriend, is in England and I'd like to find out how and when I could leave."

Henry took his sister to the harbour to make enquiries about the departure of boats. There was one in the harbour and when a sailor was asked when it was leaving, the reply was, "Soon." Charlotte decided.

"I'm going," she said, "I must get some clothes and money."

"You may be too late, we could leave at any time." There was a primitive gangplank so Charlotte scrambled aboard this old cattle ship and Henry dashed to the Hougue Père to fetch her coat, money and all the clothes her mother and sister could stuff in a suitcase. He was back in time to throw her belongings into the boat before it pulled away. In the meanwhile her boyfriend, Bob Mahy, who was employed at Vickers factory in Southampton, had received a couple of telegrams from Charlotte indicating that she might be coming to England. He lodged with Alf Ferbrache, a workmate, and his family; Bob showed him the telegrams.

"I cannot understand what is happening in Guernsey, I'm going over to find out what is going on," he said. He packed an overnight bag and went to the docks. There he saw a notice announcing that there would be no boat leaving for the Channel Islands until the next day. Very frustrated Bob returned home. The next evening he was shaving before leaving for the docks when there was a knock on the door. Charlotte had arrived. They shuddered to think that, had she arrived an hour later, Bob might have ended up trapped in Guernsey and she stranded in England.

With Charlotte and John gone, their sister Phyllis was more restless than ever and when her aunt decided to go to Plymouth, Phyllis went with her on one of the last boats to leave the island.

A fortnight later Charlotte and Bob were married in England. Charlotte bought a hat, a dress and a cake. Bob ordered a taxi and together Mr. & Mrs. Ferbrache as witnesses, they drove to a Registry Office. The taxi driver said that if there was an air raid warning he would go to a shelter, but not to worry. He would be back.

There was no air raid and when the wedding party emerged, he was waiting. They drove to the Ferbrache house and invited the friendly taxi driver to come in and have a piece of wedding cake. This was the wedding reception, a far cry from the big traditional family wedding of which Charlotte had often dreamed.

In Guernsey many young couples who were engaged to be married at some future date married hastily before going away together. Others married with the intention of evacuating but eventually changed their minds or left it too late and were trapped on the island.

On Monday June 24th, Jack Sebire was walking down the hill with his suitcase on his way to the boats intent on joining Mona his wife and infant son John, who had already evacuated.

Jack Mahy, his father-in-law, met him and said, "Haven't you heard? The tomatoes are being shipped again, everything is back to normal!" He hurried along to see to his lorry, he had a carting business and Jack Sebire turned back, changed his clothes, and picked his tomatoes.

Four days later, Jack Mahy was dead, killed during the air raid on the White Rock. Jack Sebire was trapped in Guernsey.

That Monday morning, the order, "Business as usual, pick and pack your tomatoes," put new heart into everyone.

"The Germans are not coming here after all, they've got far bigger fish to fry. What use could these small islands be to them?" we asked ourselves.

Mr. Girard and his wife, after much worrying and heart searching, decided to evacuate with their family. They were driving towards town in their van when they saw a placard placed in a conspicuous position with "STAY AT HOME. DON'T BE YELLOW" written in large letters.

Mr. Girard had an immediate change of heart and promptly turned his horse around and returned home. These placards dotted about the island must have helped to influence many undecided people to stay in Guernsey.

When wives telephoned anxiously from the mainland they were told the good news. "Shipping is resumed, we're sending tomatoes, stay where you are for a couple of weeks then I'll come and fetch you."

This false cheer lasted a week.

In the week following the evacuation it was as though the Pied Piper had passed through Guernsey and the children had followed. Some children, like Lucille, remained but the large majority were gone.

After 21,000 of Guernsey's 44,000 population were safely evacuated the authorities looked towards the lonely island of Alderney from which every man, woman and child had been ordered to leave. Before leaving the island the owners had let loose all their cattle. Now the animals were roaming over Alderney, a motley assortment of cats, dogs, rabbits, horses, pigs, steers, bulls and cows stumbling along with their swollen udders heavy with milk.

Three crack shots; a well known St. Saviour's farmer Bonamy

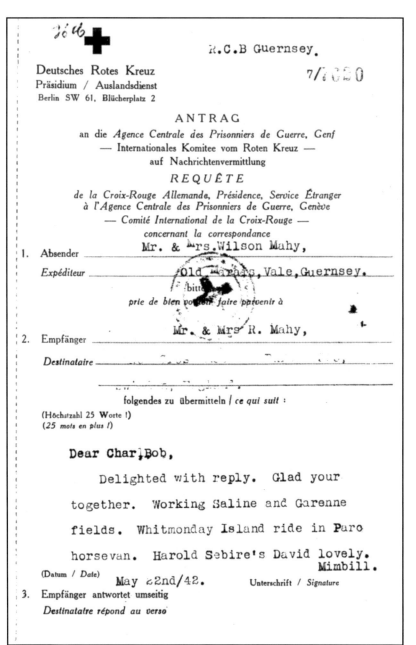

4. Antwort des Empfängers :
   Réponse du destinataire :

   (Höchstzahl 25 Worte !)
   (25 *mots au plus !*)

   Dear Mim & Bill,
   Baby is now two months
   old, wish you could see him.
   all family well, write often
   Hope see you soon Love

   PASSED
   P. 262

   (Datum / *Date*)

   C Mahy

   (Unterschrift)
   (*Signature*)

Martel, Captain Bisset and Bert Falla were among a party of men sent to Alderney to round up the animals.

The original plan was to collect all the good animals for transportation to a large farm in Cornwall. Two boats had already left Cardiff and were on their way to fetch the cattle. Sadly, both boats were sunk by the enemy. There was a hasty change of plan on the 24th June the 'Courier' and the 'Fawn' left St. Peter Port harbour with a party of men for Alderney.

All the dogs and animals not suitable for transportation, like steers and bulls, and any animals in distress, were shot. The cows were milked and gradually the finest animals were herded together ready for their journey to Guernsey. Back and forth went the gallant little boats with their loads of livestock. Their job done, the men were back home and on Friday, June 28th the last boat load of pigs was on its way to St. Peter Port. Its cargo was to be taken with the other Alderney animals to the now deserted airport, prior to being collected by island farmers.

The last load never reached St. Peter Port, the boat was machine-gunned by enemy aircraft and just managed to slip into St. Sampson's harbour.

Alf Martel was one of the men who went to Alderney. He was a big man, tall, very strong, daring, and completely fearless. His dark skin was usually unshaven, he had a loud gruff voice and a louder laugh. When the party of men left Alderney for home Alf decided to stay on alone and added humorously, "I'll be King of Alderney." His brothers in Guernsey were anxious when they heard the story, so they boarded one of the boats and went to look for him. They found him lying fully dressed on a luxurious bed in one of the hotels and surrounded by bottles of whisky. It was with difficulty that they persuaded him to come home! Alf was hauled off to prison a couple of times during the occupation but this meant nothing to him. He was a difficult person to punish because he just did not care.

Chapter 3

GUERNSEY UNDER ATTACK

It was a busy week for growers, the tomato crop was bulking and there was much picking, packing and watering to be done.

The first sense of unease came on Thursday 27th June when we saw a lone enemy aircraft fly over, the iron cross was plain to see as it flew low over the harbour. The next day, Friday 28th June, three bombers flew over and bombed the harbours, circled the island, machine-gunning as they went, then returned to the White Rock where the lorries and drivers were lined up waiting to ship the tomatoes. The safest place proved to be under the jetties. Many of the drivers who crawled under their lorries for shelter were burned or killed by skidding machine gun bullets. Some men jumped over the wall on to the beach and others were sprayed with bullets as they climbed over.

Mr. Le Page from King's Mills had taken his two small sons with him in the lorry for a treat. They died with him.

Another driver stood behind a pillar with his little boy in front of him and moved around the pillar as the aircraft circled. When it was all over he was congratulating himself that they were both safe, then he noticed that the toes of one of his feet had been shot away.

John Mahy, universally known as 'Farmer John', lived in our lane. He reached home safely and stripped to have a wash.

His father said, "Your back is bleeding," and sure enough, he was peppered with shrapnel. Bill drove him to hospital for treatment.

Fortunately Bill had taken his load of tomatoes earlier to the White Rock and was back home having tea when he heard the explosions and the continuous rat-a-tat-tat of the machine guns. We rushed outside then in again as the aircraft came roaring overhead.

*Devastation after the air raid over the harbour in June 1940 showing
the Weighbridge clock and the tomato lorries bombed on the pier.
(Photograph courtesy of Bill Gillingham)*

The attack lasted about an hour. Guernsey was an open town so we had no guns with which to retaliate.

The Bailiff and his staff stared at each other in disbelief before one of them grabbed the telephone and got through to the Home Office.

"This is Guernsey, we are being bombed."

"Impossible," was the reply, "you're an open town."

"Listen to this!" and the Bailiff held the receiver through the open window.

The only guns on the island were those on the boats loading tomatoes and these shot at the aeroplanes when they came within range. Rumours followed that British fighters were sent to intercept our German attackers and succeeded in shooting them down into the sea.

On the night of the air-raid, the telephone wires between England and Guernsey must have been red hot. Charlotte telephoned to ask her parents' permission to marry Bob. She obtained their agreement and good wishes and did not speak with them again for five years.

Our close friend, Mona Sebire, telephoned anxiously after hearing of the bombing of the Channel islands on the wireless set and was told the tragic news that her father was one of the 29 victims. Her husband and other husbands assured their wives that they were coming to England on the first available boat. Too late. There were no more boats.

Abruptly, the telephone wires were cut and communication ended.

We realised at last that we were in real trouble and that the Germans would come.

Plans were made for a second evacuation. Bill was in charge of a district which he was to notify the moment the boats arrived.

On Sunday 30th June, we had tea at 'Rockdale', my parents' home, and were taking a walk by the Druid's Altar at 'Le Dehus' when an enormous troop-carrier, with the iron cross clearly showing, flew over at such a low altitude that we felt that we could have hit it with a stone.

German Commandant's Car 1940, outside the 'Channel Islands'
Hotel'. (now demolished)

That same evening, we were walking along the Marais lane where
we lived, when we met Bill Guilliard.

"The Germans have landed," he informed us, "and the Swastika
is flying over the Royal Hotel."

Our worst fears were realised. German occupation of the Channel
Islands had begun. Silently we walked up the Hougue Père Hill to
my husband's parents' home. Never had the view been more lovely.
L'Ancresse Common was ablaze with gorse, the sea blue and calm
in the distance. The air was warm after a blazing hot day, the Vale
Church, silhouetted against the sunset, looked safe and secure as it has
stood for centuries. It did not seem possible that everything looked
the same but life had turned topsy turvy. Half our friends had gone,
parents had lost their children, the husbands who had lingered in
Guernsey to send their fruit were now frantic to evacuate but were
all trapped. Guernsey was flying the Swastika and we were under
German rule. The future loomed ahead bleak and fearful. Where life
had been happy, busy and predictable, now all was chaos, confusion
and uncertainty.

Chapter 4

RE-ORGANISING ISLAND LIFE

After the initial shock of evacuation and occupation, life began by degrees to assume some sort of pattern. The banks reopened and people grew accustomed to handling reichsmarks. The shops, though much depleted by goods by the soldiers, were still open for business.

For about a week the islanders were in a vacuum. Then the German orders were issued.

The States must organise the islanders to grow food for themselves and for the soldiers. We were about 23,000 islanders and at one time there were again as many Germans and foreign labourers.

The Glasshouse Utilization Board, or G.U.B., was formed. The headquarters were at Hirzel House, St. Peter Port, and the Vale depot was in a bungalow called 'Chelston' at Les Landes. All produce grown in the various parishes had to go through the parish depot for distribution to the shops after a percentage had been set aside for the Germans.

At this time the tomato plants that had been so carefully reared and tended by the growers were drooping with their load of ripe fruit. The greenhouses gleamed red in the sunlight and the Glasshouse Board sent men to pull up the plants and cart them to the rubbish tips.

The greenhouses were appropriated by the States. Bill was in charge of a large batch of glass at the Saline, including his own vinery, but was answerable to an overseer who in turn was accountable to the G.U.B.

The empty greenhouses were prepared for producing food for the future; carrots, turnips, potatoes, peas and beans were planted in different batches of glass.

In one vinery under his care, Bill grew thousands of little cabbage plants which, when ready to transplant, were taken to other vineries which the Glasshouse Board had chosen for growing cabbages.

Bill had mostly peas and beans growing in his greenhouses. The beans were Guernsey runners and were intended for use as green vegetables, but we dried some for winter storage. Normally nobody would have wanted to use these dried red beans for soup, but they became a luxury.

In November 1940 a Purchasing Commission which consisted of a small group of island men headed by Raymond Falla was escorted to France to buy food for the islanders.

To this day I can still see and smell on particular issue camembert cheese which was included in our weekly rations. Its odour penetrated the house and it looked more like thick cream than cheese. However, we ate it just as we hungrily ate our ration of bread from which we had first scraped the mould.

The authoress's identity card.
All islanders were issued with identity cards.

The farmers owned their cattle, but they too were under orders. They were not permitted to kill or sell their own cattle, and if a cow died or was stolen, it had to be reported immediately so that the incident could be investigated and the animal struck off the register. All children received a ration of pure milk, one pint per day, the remainder was skimmed and we received a quarter pint per person of this tasteless liquid. When an animal was slaughtered, it was compulsory for a portion of the meat to go to the Germans.

One day Harry Hamon, one of the men working on Bill's group of greenhouses, was weeding outside when Bill passed by and remarked casually, "I hear that Jack Nant had a cow stolen last night." Harry looked startled.

"When did you hear that?" he asked sharply.

"This morning," Bill replied.

Harry swore. "The fool is spreading that yarn before going to the stable and making sure. There were soldiers patrolling that area last night so we couldn't steal the cow. We were hoping to get it tonight." He hurried away to see Jack before the police came to investigate. Harry was furious; the arrangement had been that the morning after the theft, in order to allay suspicion, Jack would telephone the police and report the robbery. The plan was that the cow would be transported to a distant shed until the hue and cry had died down and then it would be slaughtered. Jack would have his share of the meat and be paid for the remainder, which would be distributed amongst Harry's friends.

Although the police had not yet been notified, Harry was worried that the story Jack had rashly told without verifying it first would reach the ears of the authorities before he and his friends had a chance to get the cow away.

The animal was duly taken the following night and the next morning there were problems with Jack Nant who proved very reluctant to report his loss.

Harry and the others threatened that Jack would not be paid, nor would he receive his share of the meat until he had telephoned the police.

German Officers in Market Square, St Peter Port 1940

As Jack had feared, when the Military Police and a local policeman arrived they were very suspicious. They questioned Jack over and over again and in his agitation, his stammering became even worse than usual but he stuck to his story. The Germans questioned the neighbours; had they seen any unusual happenings? They even dug around the property to see if they could find any remains of a slaughtered animal, but finding no evidence they were forced to give up.

Similar incidents happened all the time with the attitude "Jerry can make all the rules he likes, but in any way that we can thwart him, we shall do so."

Guernsey folk are called 'Guernsey donkeys'. I do not know where this nickname originated, but there is indeed a stubborn streak and determination in a Guernseyman allied to a fierce independence.

At this time, bureaucracy had not yet reared its ugly head, a man was free to go as he pleased and do as he wished within the law. He could sell what he liked, buy as he chose, build or demolish with very little restriction. His own was his own to do as he would. Therefore it was doubly difficult for the Guernseyman to accept a foreign power laying down rules and regulations in his own island.

Chapter 5

LIFE UNDER ENEMY RULE

At first the islanders were permitted to keep their wireless sets, we did not call them 'radios' at this time. The Germans were winning and they had nothing to hide.

Groups of soldiers would march through the town and along the roads singing their rousing German songs. The beauty of their singing would have done justice to any choir, but to us it was the most depressing sound in the world.

At the outbreak of war we had all been issued with British ration books for essential commodities. These rations were adequate, Guernsey shops and stores were stocked with goods at the beginning of the occupation, there were also all the goods brought over from Alderney and the States arranged a collection of all food left in empty houses.

Alas the soldiers, having come from France and Germany where food was scarce, were soon raiding the shops and buying everything in sight, not only food but clothing as well which they sent to their relatives at home. This meant that by Christmas the shops were virtually empty.

Rumour was rife, conversations began with "They say...." or "Have you heard.....?" "They say that all men under 30 years of age will be sent to France...." "that the Russians have joined the allies and the war will soon be over...." "that English born people are to be deported...." "that this particular group of houses is being commandeered....." that our wireless sets are to be confiscated..." and so it went on.

Soon after the Germans arrived, four soldiers went to a house at L'Ancresse and ordered the woman there to prepare them a cooked

German soldiers marching past the Town Church. A common sight on our roads at this time. (Photograph courtesy of R. K. Mahy)

meal for 6 p.m. The lady telephoned the police and was put through to the German Commandant. She asked if she was compelled to serve this meal. The reply was 'yes' but she must tell nobody that she had telephoned. At 6 p.m. the soldiers entered and an excellent meal was served. They had begun eating it when the door burst open and the German police strode in. The terrified soldiers were brutally assaulted before being dragged away. This was an example of German discipline in action.

The glorious summer seemed to mock our frustration and never more so than one beautiful Sunday in mid-September 1940. We were walking to our Methodist Church when wave after wave of German bombers roared overhead. They were coming from the Guernsey airport, the Blitz had begun and they were heading for England in perfect formation.

As we went soberly into Church, we could only pray for the victims of this formidable attack. We sang from our hearts the hymn which was sung almost every Sunday during the occupation.

'Holy Father in Thy Mercy,
Hear our anxious prayer,
Keep our loved ones now far distant,
'Neath Thy care.'

German Troops marching along North Esplanade, St Peter Port,
in August 1940.

Chapter 6

COMMUNITY SPIRIT

How can I describe the community spirit that pervaded the island? Just over half the islanders were left under the yoke of a common enemy. We had all lost relatives and friends, our cars were either hidden or had been commandeered by the enemy and the most unlikely people of all ages were riding bicycles.

Mrs. Clara McKane was a well-known figure in the Vale Parish. Every Saturday morning she harnessed her horse and set off from La Turquie, in the Vale, with a van load of passengers en route for St. Peter Port. people who did not ride bicycles were glad to avail themselves of the opportunity of a trip into town. Although there was very little to buy it was a welcome change from the daily routine. Mrs. McKane's cheerful smile and her service to the community were very much appreciated.

The banks had transferred island money and assets to England. George Orwell wrote "All men are equal but some are more equal than others." In our situation during the occupation, men were indeed equal.

There was a friendliness and warmth in people's attitudes towards each other, a caring and sharing of problems, interests and recipes! Time to know people with whom we had previously exchanged a brief "Good morning". There was time to chat in little groups outside garden gates or as we queued for fish and our meagre rations.

I remember having breakfast one morning, when Jim Stacey our milkman arrived with our pint of skimmed milk. Alf Martel had dropped in on his way to dig potatoes and soon our table was partly cleared to make room for the map of Europe. While we breakfasted they argued and worked out the war positions according to the latest news.

Everybody's common interest was the news.

It was a blow to lose our wireless sets in September 1940 as a reprisal after Lieuts. Hubert Nicolle and James Symes had landed on our south coast. They were local boys who were serving in H.M. Forces. The British landed them on the island so that they could mix with Guernsey people and find out how we were faring under Nazi rule. Arrangements had been made to pick them up again when they had obtained the information needed. Sadly, they were caught by the enemy and sent to an internment camp.

It was almost worthwhile losing the sets to know that England had not forgotten us. However, we were sad to learn that these brave lads had been captured and punished.

The sets were collected in lorries and piled in a couple of rooms at the Vale School. They were returned to us on Christmas Eve with the threat that next time German Law was broken, they would be confiscated for the duration.

Clara McKane with her horse drawn bus. (Photograph courtesy of V. Coysh and C. Toms)

There were air raids by the British on the airport, harbours and gun emplacements. We lived near L'Ancresse Common and one night we could hear some popping noises outside, so we went out to investigate and stood there looking upward wondering where these strange sounds came from, then dashed quickly inside as we realised that an English plane had just flown over and the L'Ancresse anti-aircraft guns were firing at it. The noise was shrapnel dropping around us.

My father watched what transpired to be a British fighter high in the sky, then a German aeroplane flew overhead. It seemed to him that the British fighter lingered until the enemy was over the sea then, like a hawk, down he swooped. There was the noise of gunfire and the German twisted over and over and down into the sea.

Another time, Bill was standing with the Dean Rev. Frossard, watching a dogfight overhead. It lasted quite a while, the fighters weaving and turning and twisting until, finally, there was a cloud of smoke and one of them fell like a stone into the sea. It was impossible to tell which was the victor or vanquished. The awesome spectacle over, Rev. Frossard and Bill turned away and soberly went their separate ways, the same thought uppermost in their minds, "There was a man in that 'plane."

The Germans later received a message that three British aircraft were heading for Guernsey so they prepared their guns. At the White Rock, a Guernseyman stood and watched three aeroplanes flying very low as they approached the island. There was a bark of gunfire and they were hit.

After the first jubilant cheer from the watching Germans, consternation reigned. A ghastly mistake had been made. The three British fighters had indeed arrived but were flying very high over head while three German aircraft were coming in flying very low to avoid the fighters, only to be shot down by their own men.

The watching Guernseyman laughed and laughed and was promptly arrested and taken to gaol by the irate enemy.

On another occasion, three British bombers flew low over the Island. Bill and his fellow workers at the vinery hastily climbed up on the flat roofed packing shed to follow their flight.

The aeroplanes flew towards town at a terrific speed and the men heard three bombs explode and commented, "They'll never hit anything flying at that speed, it's impossible to aim straight at a target."

German anti aircraft gun at L'Ancresse Bay.

We heard the next day that three bombs had indeed been dropped, one on the pier, one straight into the hold of a ship and the other on one side of it.

The Germans were reputed to have declared that they wished they had those pilots fighting on their side. Their aim was so accurate.

Chapter 7

ISLAND SCHOOLS

The island parish schools reopened on July 15th 1940. Five thousand children and most of their teachers had evacuated so the schools were staffed by the few teachers who had remained in the island, retired teachers, clergymen and volunteers from among the general public. In the same way many nurses at this time were also recruited from retired professionals or people with some nursing experience. The pupils of the Colleges and the Intermediate schools initially attended these parish schools so there was a very wide age range.

The Castel and the Vale Schools had the largest number of pupils. At the first assembly, Castel School had 159 children, the Vale had 120. Mr. Peter Girard was appointed Head of Castel School and Mrs. Amy Veal, Head of the Vale School. Shortly afterwards, Mrs. Veal became ill and Mrs. Millicent Gale took her place after having left the profession in 1928 when her first baby was born.

The Vale Infant School building was being used as a potato depot, so the school was housed in the Junior School building. The new school was just well organised when in strode a German official who confronted Mrs. Gale with the command, "You are to be out of the premises by 12 o'clock. We need the school for a hospital."

Another venue had to be found so the trustees of the nearby Methodist Church gave permission for the Vale School to use the Church schoolrooms for lessons.

According to the Geneva Convention all children in occupied territories had to be weighed once a month. If a child lost weight a ration of cod liver oil was supplied. Every first Friday of the month the children were stripped of the bulk of their clothing and weighed. Each morning the milkman called at the school with a can of full cream milk for the children. Their ration was half a pint for each child and was served in a jam jar.

In April 1941, Mr. Peter Girard was appointed Headmaster of the Occupation Intermediate School. The result of this was that he was simultaneously Head of the Castel and Intermediate Schools and had to commute between the two on his bicycle.

There were 68 boys and girls at the new Intermediate School which was formed by a combination of former College and Intermediate pupils and other children selected by examination from parish schools.

Initially the Intermediate School was situated in Rosaire Avenue. When this building was commandeered the school moved to Notre Dame in Burnt Lane, St. Peter Port, but, after the British had fired on the harbour, the children had to move once again, this time to a country house 'La Haye du Puits' in the Castel Parish.

At first there were more girls than boys and Mr. Girard recalls hearing the cry, "Joan, don't forget football practice at playtime."

Mr. Girard also tells how the President of the Education Council introduced him to a German who claimed to be a German teacher anxious to improve his knowledge of English and asked to be permitted to 'sit in' during lessons at the Castel School.

Later Mr. Girard was unofficially informed by a policeman that the man was a member of the Gestapo. In fact, he was a member of the 'Feldgendarmarie' who were the German Police in Guernsey, but commonly called Gestapo by Guernsey people. Once warned, everyone was careful with conversation and information.

Ten years later Peter Girard received a letter from the German apologising and confessing that he had been installed in the school as a spy. Mr. Girard promptly wrote back saying he had been well aware of the fact at the time. In his letter the German had explained that his conduct had not met with the approval of the Nazi authorities and he had therefore been deported to Russia and had suffered terrible hardship. From this story we see how the Germans constantly disrupted all aspects of island life. However, although they commandeered school buildings without warning and children were moved again and again, their education continued under the dedicated care of their teachers. In fact, after five years of occupation, the Guernsey children were more than able to hold their own with those who returned from England.

Vale Mill, used by the Germans as observation post with 3 extra floors.

Chapter 8

CLEARING ALDERNEY

Herbert Perchard, better known as 'Ginger', was a garage mechanic but he had served in the Army Medical Corps, so after the air raid he worked for a while as an orderly at the hospital.

In September he was summoned to the 'States Essential Commodities' at the Ladies' College to see Deputy R.H. Johns and Rev. Philip Romeril who were in charge of labour. He was asked to supervise twenty men who were being sent to Alderney to collect all perishable goods that could be used by Guernsey people.

The boat was manned by Germans who escorted the Guernseymen to Fort Albert and left them there for three days while they searched the island. Some old people who had previously refused to leave home were now taken to Guernsey where they were housed in the Victoria Homes. The animals that had been missed on the first visit were running wild and were shot.

The Guernsey workers were then lodged in Alderney's Grand Hotel where they lived for several months.

Alderney was well stocked with a three year supply of goods. A further ten men were brought over and gradually the houses were emptied of supplies as were the shops and stores and their contents were transported to Guernsey. Sacks of flour and sugar and all the coal was taken to St. Peter Port. Meanwhile, the grain was harvested and potatoes were dug.

When Bert Perchard returned home, he brought the film projector from the Alderney Cinema and all the films that were there. These became very popular and Bert was always ready to entertain groups of school children with a film show. His fame spread and people invited him into their homes to give film shows for their friends.

The Germans were unaware of these activities until Bert was caught by a German patrol at an all night party at Grandes Rocques. There were fifty people laughing uproariously at the antics of George Formby strumming his banjo. The noise was deafening, the Germans charged in, hauled Bert off to prison and left him there for five days while they examined his films.

Alderney Harbour, June 1940, after the evacuation of all Alderney residents.

Ginger was released. He was fiery with a temper to match his hair and he was furious at the loss of his films. He stalked angrily into the 'gendarmerie' and demanded his property. He was refused, so undaunted, he went to the Kommandant headquarters and explained that he had promised to give a children's Christmas Show and needed his projector and films.

The Germans decided that the films were old and harmless and after some discussion he was given a permit to show them. He was warned that if he dared show them again after curfew there would be trouble. Bert happily wheeled his equipment home in a handcart and, ignoring the threat, continued showing his films to all those who invited him.

Chapter 9

COMMANDEERING HOUSES

Roland Guille had a farm at the Fauxquets Valley. The Germans commandeered his stables to house some of their horses. One particular horse was very troublesome, it would rear up on its hind legs and stamp about when anyone approached it with the result that the soldiers were terrified and when they fed the horse they would rush in, fling the food before it and rush out again while the animal made a terrible fuss.

When everyone had gone Roland tried a little experiment. He held some food before the horse in a tin and, keeping a careful eye on it, he approached very quietly and gently, making sure that the animal could see him. The horse moved uneasily but Roland came on slowly and smoothly and gave it the food. He repeated the process for a few days until the horse knew him and was not nervous.

The next day, Roland said scornfully to the soldiers, "You know nothing about horses, I'm certain that I could feed that animal without making all that fuss."

"You feed him then," said one soldier handing over the dish, "and we shall see what happens." Roland took the food and confidently went forward, fed the horse, patted it fearlessly and returned triumphant to the wide-eyed soldiers.

On another occasion Roland was furious that the enemy had taken possession of his handcart so one night he removed the wheels and hid them in the hay barn deep among the bales of hay. The Germans enquired and searched for them everywhere, Roland's heart missed a beat when he saw the enemy hunting in the hay barn amongst the hay. However the wheels were never found by them and Roland continued sabotaging German equipment whenever the opportunity arose.

One day in the early months of the occupation, Edward and Eileen Collas were visited by a German officer who was accompanied by a Guernsey custodian. The German had come to view the house with the intention of commandeering it. They went into every room and the German, who was very polite and also spoke perfect English, enquired how long they had been married and when he was told four years he just nodded and made a few notes, bade them good morning and left.

The custodian told them later that the officer had remarked that the house and its contents were new and much too good for soldiers. He went to visit another house and took that instead.

Alas Edward and Eileen were not so lucky on the next occasion. This time they were given notice by the custodian that a German officer was coming to see their house. Family and friends rallied around and carried their beautiful bedroom suite to Edward's mother's house at the Tertre and replaced it with an antiquated one that had belonged to an old aunt.

I must admit that it did look incongruous on the pale fawn fitted carpet in the newly decorated room. We went around the house removing and replacing as much as we dared.

When the custodian arrived he brought with him an officer who was the complete antithesis of the previous one. He could not speak English and had an interpreter with him. They were both rough and ill mannered. The interpreter shouted the officer's queries and comments as though everyone was deaf.

On entering the guest bedroom the officer roared with laughter, then he began shouting in rapid German. Edward was commanded to return all furniture that had been removed, the furniture that fitted the dents in the carpet! All that was permitted to be removed from the house were their clothes and personal belongings. A guard was stationed outside to see that these orders were obeyed. The bedroom suite had to come back, but Edward replaced the new mattress with an old one, and other items that had been removed were left at the Tertre.

Edward was allowed to continue cultivating the garden at 'Hougue Ricart' and one day he observed a German soldier looking furtive and hiding something under a bush. That night after dark Edward crept into the garden to look for what had been hidden. He found food which he took home to add to the family rations. Soon afterwards he was banned from the garden.

Roland Guille's Farm at the Fauxquets de Bas

Jack Jehan was also ordered to evacuate his house for German occupation. The house on the opposite side of the road was empty but they did not want that one, they wanted Jack's. However, he was permitted to take his furniture and was given two hours to move it into the house opposite where he was going to live. Bill and several other friends went to help him. There was utter confusion because at the same time soldiers were moving furniture from the other house into Jack's house. Chaos reigned. Some furniture was travelling backwards and forwards between the two houses. Eventually someone contacted German headquarters and the soldiers were called away for two hours.

Chapter 10

SOCIAL EVENTS

The mellow summer days of 1940 drifted into autumn and the first occupation Christmas was upon us. Our cupboards were depleted but not yet bare. While there was food in the shops the islanders saved their personal stores.

Christmas Day was spent as always with my parents at 'Rockdale'. My sisters were there and we still exchanged gifts and played Christmas games.

My mother rifled her store of food and produced two good meals. All that we provided for the party was our ration of bread. We all agreed that we must make the best of this occupation Christmas because next year the war would be over. Indeed each subsequent Christmas we would repeat the same forecast as we are our beans and parsnip cake, and added that it would be impossible to survive another year, but we were to survive four more.

During those war years when we went out for a meal the table would be set and when we entered the hostess would indicate each person's place so that we could put our bread on the side plate provided. There was usually one cake carefully cut into portions so that everyone had one piece each. The ingredients depended upon what was available. Sometimes potato flour was used and occasionally wheat gleaned from the fields at harvest and ground into flour with a coffee grinder. Providing the cake was always a small sacrifice.

Bill's father had a billiard table at the 'Hougue Père' and the men spent many hours playing billiards and snooker while his mother, Eileen, Rose, Henry and I would knit or sew and enjoy each other's company. Saturday evenings were usually spent in this way and the games became very competitive and much good humoured banter would ensue. Jack Sebire, Len Tupper and Tom Henry often joined in these Saturday gatherings with Henry, Edward Collas and Bill.

Electricity and water were shut off at specified times during the day. My sister-in-law, Eileen, had been out one afternoon and when she returned water was cascading down her stairs. She had hopefully turned on a tap before leaving and found that the water had already been shut off, so she went away without turning the tap off again.

On Friday nights, Henry, Bill and I went to tea at 'Le Parc' with Jack Sebire and his mother-in-law Julia and afterwards we played rummy or five hundred. We usually slept there and cycled home on Saturday morning. If we wanted refreshments during the evening we would eat a slice of swede instead of sweets or chocolate.

It is surprising how one came to terms with hunger. It was several months before we were at rock bottom rations; we reached that stage very gradually.

When our friends Len and Clara Tupper were married on April 14th 1941, Clara remembers that her first bill for housekeeping was four pence halfpenny. She had 2ozs. salt and 2ozs barley flour. However the wedding was a highlight after a gloomy winter. Tom Henry was best man and Irene Falla was bridesmaid. There were three horse traps, one for the bride and groom, another for the best man and bridesmaid and the other for the parents. The guests either walked or came on bicycles to the Vale Methodist Church.

Clara looked charming in a blue dress and matching hat, she carried a bouquet of anemones held together with a multicoloured ribbon tied in a large bow.

When Clara entered the church porch she took an instant dislike to the bow and to the bridesmaid's horror began undoing it saying impatiently, "I don't want all that frill swirling around me."

She had not bargained for the fact that the whole bouquet was wired, which caused complications. Suddenly they realised that the church organ had now burst into the first chords of 'The Wedding March'. Hurriedly Irene retied the offending bow as well as she could before following Clara and her father into the church towards the bridegroom and waiting minister.

After the ceremony the guests made their way to the wedding reception held at Le Hautgard, Clara's parents' home, and the home of the bridal couple for the duration of the war. There was even a wedding cake. Clara's mother had saved all the ingredients she could manage for the occasion. Relatives had helped, one supplying a few currants, another a handful of raisins, until there was enough for Lena to make the cake. Lena, who had worked for the family all her life, was an excellent cook. She also rummaged in her cupboards and emerged triumphant with a tin containing ground almonds which she brought to Le Hautgard.

They looked at the ground almonds doubtfully, they were certainly old and speckled with green mould. Clara carefully picked out and threw away the green bits and the rest made excellent almond paste for the wedding cake. There were also sandwiches and little cakes. We were able to drink the health of the bride and bridegroom in champagne which Clara's father brought from Jethou.

He was able to do this because, when the house in Jethou, previously occupied by Compton McKenzie, was emptied of its contents Deputy H.J. Bichard, Clara's father, supervised the operation. When he had seen the champagne there he sought and received permission from the authorities to buy a few bottles for the wedding day.

Photographs were taken in the garden and Clara and Len stepped into their horse and trap which took them to Len's bungalow at St. Martin's where they spent their wedding night.

After their short honeymoon in St. Martin's, the newly-weds returned to Le Hautgard. Clara's mother produced a chicken which was a tremendous treat and a neighbour turned up with three eggs which Clara boiled for tea. One of them was bad!

Chapter 11

ESCAPES

Guernsey settled down to life under enemy rule. There were several men and girls working at Bill's vinery at the Saline. They were engaged in clearing old crops and planting new.

Conversation would invariably revert to what was happening in England. There was always debate and discussion about the progress of the war especially about where there had been bombing the previous night. There was much anxiety when there were reports of bombing near the areas where evacuated wives and families were living.

In 1941 the Red Cross organised the sending of Red Cross messages to and from England. It was sometimes months before the brief censored messages were received but at least they informed the Guernsey evacuees that their relatives were surviving and we found out where our friends were living.

Many of the men weighed the pros and cons of escaping to England and discussed leaving the island in a fishing boat, but nobody took them seriously.

Among the men working at the Saline was Fred Hockey who, like many others, had lingered for too long after his wife and child's departure. One day in early September Fred waited until Bill was alone and, swearing him to secrecy, explained how he and seven others were planning to escape from Bordeaux at midnight that night. It was going to be a risky business and Bill shook hands with Fred and wished him well.

The following morning Bill cycled to the vinery wondering what comments the others would make on Fred's non-appearance, when the first person he met was Fred Hockey. What an anti climax!

"Why are you here? What happened?" was Bill's greeting. Fred was not pleased.

"Bert Bichard flatly refused to leave because the German patrol boat was around and he claimed that it was too dangerous. We've warned him," Fred continued, "that if he hangs back tonight, whatever happens, we will take the boat without him."

The following morning, Fred did not arrive for work and Bill made no comment. Later in the day there were stories of a boat missing from Bordeaux and Fred's workmates were not long before putting two and two together. Speculation and rumour began.

The Germans were furious and stopped permits for fishing. An order was published in the 'Press' stating that all boats in the island had to be in the town harbour by a given date. This was particularly hard on the west coast fishermen who had to bring their boats across the island to the harbour as best they could. A warning was published stating that, should there be any more escapes, reprisals would be taken again the Guernsey people, and males of military age would be taken to France.

We learned much later that Fred Hockey and his comrades left Bordeaux without incident and reached the Platte Fougère lighthouse at 12.30 a.m. when a German aircraft flew over and dropped a flare. Terrified, the men lay flat on the bottom of the boat and held their breath. It was like daylight until the flare burnt out and the men could not understand why they were not seen. They continued the hazardous journey and a 4 a.m. their engine broke down. This was repaired and on they went. It was foggy which made navigation difficult, but on the credit side the fog was a cloak that hid them from the enemy.

They sighted land at Start Point in Devon and anchored at Berry Head at 6 p.m. the following day after a nineteen hour journey in a 21ft. open boat.

The men were escorted to a Merchant Home where they remained under guard all night. Next morning they were driven to Plymouth and interviewed at the Town Hall. The next step was the Police Station where they were all issued with permits and sent on their way to seek their wives.

Bill Lawrence was another man who worked on Bill's vinery. He was using a bicycle belonging to us. One morning the cycle was by our back door with no word of explanation. We immediately surmised that Lawrence had escaped from the island and did not want to involve us. Sure enough a fishing boat was missing and he was one of the missing persons. That night a terrible storm arose and the Germans declared that they would not take reprisals on the islanders because the occupants of a small fishing boat could not possibly escape drowning in those heavy seas.

After the war Bill Lawrence told of his nightmare journey. One person just lay in the water on the bottom of the boat too ill to move. The others baled out and hoped and baled and tossed to and fro on the angry waves until luckily an English warship picked them up out of the storm and took them to England.

Fred Hockey and his brother Harold forty years later at Bordeaux harbour from which they escaped in a small boat in October 1940. (Photograph courtesy of The Guernsey Evening Press and Star)

Chapter 12

CURFEW

After a while we accepted the fact of occupation. There was nothing we could do about the situations so we adjusted our lives to it. We soon grew accustomed to double summer time and to the curfew which at first was 11 p.m. and then changed to 10 p.m. and then 9 p.m.

We made our own entertainment and visited each other, sometimes staying to sleep but often ignoring the curfew and coming home very late. Many times Bill and I jumped over a hedge and hid while the German patrol passed by. The noise of the soldiers' jack boots and their guttural voices gave due warning of their approach. Sometimes we could have touched them as they passed.

One moonlight night we were walking along Les Landes when we spied German soldiers in the distance so we got behind a high wall. Bill had another peep and noticed that the patrol was accompanied by alsation dogs. We did not waste a moment but hurried to a house and waited there until the party had passed by before continuing home.

Another night, returning from a party, we heard footsteps at a distance behind us. Bill said, "Come on, over the wall." A wave of rebellion swept over me.

"No," I replied, "I'm not moving away from this road." Bill urged me not to be silly, this gesture would result in us being taken to town and it was very late! "I don't care, this is my road, my island and I'm not moving for any German, why should I?"

Bill shrugged philosophically, "If that's how you feel, we stay." We walked slowly and the steps came closer and closer until a lone officer strode past us, his cape flicking Bill's arm as he went by. He did not utter a word. Nor did we.

Every Wednesday evening a fellowship meeting was held at Salem

Chapel near L'Islet. It was always an enjoyable, friendly gathering with quite a crowd of people as the L'Islet Salvation Army had joined Salem. When the Germans had arrived they disbanded the Salvation Army, which, because of its militant name, was forbidden to meet. Uniforms and instruments were hidden away and members joined other denominations in their worship.

If you have never been out on a dark winter night, without a star in the sky, a street lamp or a light from a window, then you cannot know what it means not to be able to see your hand in front of your face.

On such a night we talked for a few minutes to friends outside the gate and somehow we started home on the wrong road. We thought we knew where we were and walked on in the pitch black night. After a while, we could not feel any hedge on either side of the road. We did not know where we were and by this time the road was rough and grassy. Suddenly I saw a tiny flicker of light to the left of us. We stumbled on towards it and found a hedge and a gate and eventually a door. We had crossed the main L'Islet road and were on the common walking towards the beach and the sea. When we realised where we were, we made our way back to the main road and slowly found our way home.

We lived in the Old Marais Lane and in this road there lived a family which German soldiers would visit. Further along on the same side lived old Mr and Mrs Guillard. Their sons, Wilson and Eugene, would often visit their parents in the evening. They knew that the Germans were sometimes at the other cottage and so they would deliberately stroll past ten minutes before the 9 o'clock curfew. They knew that the enemy would be waiting to catch them on their way back after the curfew so they would nip through the back garden and the field behind and back home before 9 o'clock while the soldiers watched and waited in vain.

Chapter 13

POLICE

In their capacity as policemen, the Guernsey Police had access to places forbidden to civilians and one night in 1941 eight or nine policemen invaded the market and stole meat and other food for themselves and their families.

They were suspected by the German authorities and apprehended. One of them was escorted to his own garden by the Military Police and forced to dig it thoroughly because the enemy had reason to believe that he had buried food there. No food was discovered. He was made to dig the patch again and again until at last his resistance snapped and he dug up the food.

The accused policemen were tried by the German court and deported to concentration camps from which some of them never returned.

During their interrogation, one young Guernsey policeman was accused by the Germans of driving the get-away vehicle for the police. He vehemently protested his innocence. The two Germans stood one each side of him and each time he denied having driven, one German punched him towards the other, who promptly hit him back from the other side and so forth until the poor young man was completely disorientated and finally blurted out, "But I can't drive!"

"Why didn't you say so before?" was his tormentors' retort.

When P.C. O'Donovan joined the Police Force in 1942 there were just over thirty policemen. He told me that one of his duties was supervising the queue at the vegetable market on ration days. He said that pregnant women were always permitted to go ahead of the queue. One day an indignant lady in the queue complained to P.C. O'Donovan that it was not fair that a certain women had jumped the queue.

"Can't you see she's pregnant?" replied the policeman.

"Rubbish," retorted the complainant, "she's got a cushion under her skirt."

It was an awkward moment for the policeman.

After the accused had been served he spoke to her quietly, saying that he was not accusing her, but it was suspected that she was cheating and that dishonesty did not pay and he advised her to be careful in the future.

As a Guernsey policeman it was easy to get into awkward situations. One night as P.C. O'Donovan was on the beat in Bosq Lane, he met a local man whom he knew well coming out of a house after curfew. He looked as though he had imbibed too freely. He was a pleasant chap and P.C. O'Donovan did not want him to get into trouble so he offered to escort him to his home.

All went well until they reached a German store with a sentry on guard. That was the moment when the man burst into song and 'There'll always be an England' rang through the still air. Fortunately either the sentry did not recognise the song or, still more likely, did not speak English.

Whenever possible the local police would help or shield their fellow islanders from the enemy.

Chapter 14

ENTERTAINMENT

Before the war, the Vale Methodist Church was a very active church with a large Sunday School. After the evacuation there were very few children left and many parents had evacuated as well. However many previous 'non-church goers' joined us and there was always a large congregation.

Our minister, Rev. Sydney Beaugie, sent his daughter to join his family in England but elected to remain with us in Guernsey to face whatever the future held. We appreciated this sacrifice. We were also fortunate to have Wilfred Corbet as organist and choirmaster, and on special occasions the Capelles choir would amalgamate with the Vale and the church was always filled to capacity for those concerts. It was an inspiring experience to join in the singing with such a congregation.

After the usual Sunday service the young people, including my sister Hazel who was eighteen at that time, would gather in the schoolroom for a social hour when they could eat the sandwich they had brought from home and someone would make carrot tea. Then they would have different sorts of entertainment.

The ladies of the church met weekly on Wednesday afternoons. A speaker was invited to give a brief talk on a religious subject or some other topic of interest and a pleasant hour was spent together.

Other churches held similar meetings usually on a Tuesday or Wednesday afternoon and I was often invited as speaker at these assemblies. I would have to set off fairly early, especially if the weather was rough or if it was raining. After a time my bicycle, like those of my friends, was fitted with hose pipe tyres and, although it went beautifully downhill, riding uphill or against the wind was hard going.

On a bad day it was easier to dismount, push the bicycle and walk rather than cycling against the wind.

At first the Vale Recreation Club continued functioning every Wednesday evening as it had before the war. Badminton and table tennis were played in the schoolrooms with chess or draughts for those who wanted them. After the Germans had commandeered the nearby Vale School, and the children continued their education in the Vale Methodist premises, the club was obliged to change its venue to the Church Hall halfway down the 'Croix du Bois' hill until the enemy also claimed those premises and there was nowhere else to go.

Hazel and her contemporaries played tennis on the tennis courts at the Rocque Balan in the summer and netball in winter. They all joined Mary Balfour's weekly dancing classes which were much enjoyed.

To organise a dance was forbidden, but the young people held private parties where there was dancing. Two large private houses which were popular for parties were 'Sunnycroft' in the Grange and 'The Grove' in Military Road. All entertainments closed in time for people to reach their homes before curfew unless they were private all night parties.

After one of these we cycled home after 6 a.m. when curfew ended and stumbled exhausted into bed. We were awakened by an imperative shout outside our window.

"Bill, Bill, Bill!" continued the unrelenting voice.

Bill wearily drew back the curtains and there stood his grandfather.

"Aren't you up yet? It's nearly 8 o'clock and I need you to wheel my loaded wheelbarrow to my house now." There was only one thing to do. Bill got up.

The island was fortunate to have two companies of local actors, The Regal Players and The Old Amherstians. We looked forward eagerly to their three act play productions which were always excellent and produced at the Old Lyric Theatre.

Variety shows by local artists were very popular. These were usually held in the Central Hall or, during the summer, in the Candie

Auditorium. Freda and Daphne Brache or 'The Brache Sisters' as they were called, were great favourites. They sang in the style of the Andrews Sisters accompanied by their father at the piano. They were always in great demand throughout the island by anyone preparing a concert. Peter Campbell was a popular compère and comedian as was Len Winterflood.

There proved to be an amazing amount of talent in the Island. Bert Hewlett and his 'Sarnia Harmonica Band', all dressed in green and white, was another much sought after act. Another well supported recreation was roller skating at St George's Hall.

The Gaumont Cinema in St Julian's Avenue was open throughout the occupation. During the war there was a barrier in the centre, on one side of which sat the soldiers, with civilians on the other. There were usually two Germans and one local policeman on guard.

We had lost or freedom, there were hardships that we would never have believed possible but, within the limits of occupation, we made our fun and created our own entertainment.

This is one of my poetic efforts written for performance at a party:

Before the War

We dieted to get so slim,
Our nightmare was a double chin.
Now we have to take in slack,
Or cotton wool in corset pack.

In our cars we used to glide,
Wireless sets we had, McMichaels.
Cats whiskers we now must hide
Have rubber hoses on our cycles.

In wind or storm we felt all right
Elastic kept our clothes on tight,
With safety pins that jingle under,
We still have faith but sometimes wonder!

We used to talk of fruit in tins,
And spring clothes each year new.
Now we talk of vitamins
And German Persian stew.

Before the war we used to spurn
The folk who were too old to learn.
The value now we truly know
Of peace and freedom here below.

Regal Cinema (now demolished) in Upland Road.

Chapter 15

DECEIVING THE ENEMY

There was a Frenchman who was billeted at L'Ancresse Lodge. He had called at our house a few times asking for food and we had given him a little. One day he arrived with about £20 worth of German reichsmarks and a large trunk, explaining that he would be away from the Lodge for a while and would Bill please look after these possessions which he feared would be stolen if left there. There was one small snag. He had lost the key and would Bill try to open the trunk please?

"Certainly," was the reply. "The only thing to do is ignore the lock and force open the hinges at the bottom." The trunk was soon open and the Frenchman was delighted. While he rummaged through the contents he came upon a cigar which he offered to Bill. This was treasure indeed and it was reverently handed over to me to hide in a safe place until Christmas Eve, to be savoured as a special treat.

Later, two Dutchmen called saying that they had followed the Frenchman with the trunk. They declared that it belonged to their friend and had been stolen while he was in prison. Bill was furious to have become involved in this situation.

"Come tomorrow at 5 o'clock, bring the Frenchman and I'll return the trunk to its owner."

Only the Dutch boys arrived the next day and Bill handed over the trunk. Nobody mentioned the money, goodness knows where it had come from.

Sometime later the Frenchman arrived asking for food and was informed by Bill in no uncertain terms that the trunk had been returned to its rightful owner.

"Never come here again," Bill said. "Take your money and go."

So the man went.

There is a sequel to this story.

When Christmas Eve arrived and we were settling down for the evening Bill said expectantly, "I've waited a long time and here's Christmas Eve. I'll have my cigar now, so please get it from its hiding place."

My heart plummeted. I had never given the cigar a second thought and worse still I just could not remember where I had put it! I made no reply but left the room and began frantically searching high and low until I eventually I was forced to admit that the much longed for cigar was lost. Months later it turned up behind some pillowslips looking crumbled and pathetic. I suppose Bill learnt a lesson. Never put off until tomorrow what you can smoke today!

In the case of the Frenchman and the trunk we were the target for the Frenchman's duplicity. However, it was more usual for people to try to outwit the Germans.

Harold Gilroy had permission to use his tractor for ploughing patches of ground in preparation for planting potatoes and vegetables. He also collected vraic from the beach in his old Ford lorry. He had a permit for a small allocation of petrol and a bigger ration of paraffin. The tractor only needed a little petrol to start it off and then it would go forever on paraffin.

Harold knew a man who drove a lorry for the Germans. This fellow stole German petrol and sold it to Harold, who not only used it for himself but also passed some on to a couple of local doctors whose petrol allowances was woefully inadequate for their needs.

One day, Harold was appalled to see two German cars driving into his property and for one wild moment he thought, "The German Petrol, I must quickly tip it up or get rid of it somehow."

There was no time.

"Show us where you keep your fuel!" demanded a guttural voice.

Harold produced his petrol permit and, shaking in his boots, he had no choice but to lead the way to the shed.

The first German was arrogant and offensive but the other was of a different calibre; he was quiet and Harold thought hopefully that he almost looked sympathetic. They gazed at the barrels in the shed, several barrels. The first German flicked off his glove, turned a tap, poured the liquid over the glove and smelt it.

"This is German benzine," he snapped.

Harold shook his head and protested that it was not German petrol, but his own lawful allocation. The second officer sniffed at the glove in his turn and looked doubtful, he said he could not be certain that it was German.

Harold's spirit rose a little but dropped again when the first German turned on him furiously declaring that he knew it was German benzine and asking why there was such a plentiful supply of it.

By this time Harold's father had come in and spoken indignantly in defence of his son. He was present when Harold explained that his tractor had been in a garage for repairs but he had had to leave it there and wait until the garage owner was able to get spare parts. In the meantime his petrol ration had accumulated.

The German Officer laughed in disbelief and ordered the two Gilroys into one of the cars. Harold took an opportunity to mutter to his father in Guernsey patois,

"Say as little as possible, just stick to my story."

They expected to be driven directly to town but the car left Pleinheaume and travelled along past the Vale Church along L'Ancresse Road and when they reached La Rochelle the old man was alarmed.

"Ch'est pour Paradis," he said. They were driving in the direction of Paradis and Paradis House and he was aware that it was a prison notorious for the cruelty meted out. It was a relief when the car turned towards Bordeaux and town.

Harold and his father were detained for questioning at the Gendarmerie for the whole day. They kept to their story. In fact there was a vestige of truth in Harold's explanation. When the German police enquired at Harold's garage, they were informed that the Gilroy tractor had indeed been in for repairs and had been kept there waiting for spare parts.

The Gilroys were eventually released and later discovered that the Germans had received an anonymous letter advising them to investigate the source of the Gilroy petrol. Harold always believed that they owed their release to the second German officer who had been sympathetic towards their dilemma.

Some very fine horses were stabled in the Vale Parish at La Hougue Stables. A German soldier liked his job in charge of these horses. One day he was questioned by an officer about the make and performance of his gun. His replies were unsatisfactory, the result being that the soldier was removed from his duties and sent to learn about guns. The Germans were very thorough.

At first we were depressed as we listened to groups of soldiers singing as they marched but as time went on we discovered that if a soldier neglected to sing, or sang half heartedly, he would be forced to run round and round the group as they marched and sang.

My cousin George Le Masurier, who owned a farm in Jersey, was warned by a neighbour that the Germans were searching the farms in that vicinity for pigs that they suspected were being kept by the farmers for their own larder.

George hastily summoned one of his men and together they managed to get his pigs into a covered cart. He then instructed the man to drive around Jersey all day. When the driver returned the Germans had come and gone again so the pigs went back to their sty and the enemy had been fooled. However, not everyone managed to outwit the Germans.

One day I was walking along by my father's vinery when I heard a loud explosion coming from nearby Hougue Nermont and wondered what had happened.

Two brothers, Harry and René Hamon, often took a short cut home across the minefield on the Hougue. They knew a safe path. The enemy must have become aware of this habit and altered the position of the mines. René trod on one. It blew sideways and hit Harry. René was frantic.

"I'll get a doctor."

"I've had it Ren," murmured the dying Harry. Nevertheless Dr. William Fox was contacted and came immediately. René later said that Dr. Fox did not hesitate. He strode across to Harry ignoring the fact that there were probably mines lying around and ministered to him as well as he could. Sadly, Harry died.

One Guernsey person who became famous for her opposition to the Germans was Marie Ozanne. She had attained the rank of Major in the Salvation Army at an unusually early age.

In June 1940 Marie was on a visit to her parents in Guernsey when the Nazis occupied the island. On 19th January 1941 the order came that the Salvation Army must close, all instruments and uniforms were to be discarded. The German High Command declared there was only one army, the German Army.

The following day Marie was standing, a frail young woman dressed in her uniform outside the Citadel doors with her Bible. She would go into town, still wearing her uniform, and read the Bible in the market place and in the Arcade until, eventually, her uniform was confiscated and she was warned against breaking German Regulations. Marie continued protesting against injustice and cruelty. When a Guerseyman was caught writing 'V' signs on the walls and was sent to prison, Marie offered to go in his place but this offer was refused with another warning.

She was distressed by the screams of human agony which came from Paradis prison and continually wrote letters of concern to protest to the Commandant. These were ignored but she carried on protesting against the cruel treatment meted out to prisoners.

On a bleak January day when she was reading her Bible in the Arcade, Marie was arrested and put in prison. She became very weak and started suffering severe stomach pains which her captors ignored. These pains increased until she finally collapsed. Once she was in this serious condition she was freed and sent to her parents' home but was there only a few days before being moved to hospital where she died of peritonitis on February 25th 1943 at the age of 37 years.

After the war on 23rd November 1947 General Albert Osborne attended a memorial service of thanksgiving at St. Sampson's Citadel

Marie Ozanne who died after release from prison in February 1943.

where he presented the posthumous award of 'Order of the Founder' to the memory of Major Marie Ozanne. This decoration is the highest award bestowed by the Salvation Army. It is rarely awarded and Marie Ozanne's mother was sad yet proud to receive it in remembrance of her daughter's courage.

Chapter 16

INVENTIVE COOKING

After spending some time living with Bill's parents at the Hougue Père we returned to our own home at the Marais. Looking back it was surprising how we learned to accept hunger as a natural state. At night we would often dream of food and wake up feeling hungrier than ever.

One night Bill said, "I just cannot sleep, I'm going downstairs to eat tomorrow morning's piece of bread. I can work when I'm hungry but I just can't sleep." Next morning he only had lettuce and carrot tea before going off to work on his bicycle. The early part of the year was the leanest time. The winter stock of vegetables was finished and we were waiting for spring crops.

We stored our vegetables behind the wardrobe in the bedroom for safety and slices of swede or carrot were very welcome during the evening.

The old furze ovens came into their own. Their owners cleaned them out, gathered furze from the common and many people would arrive with their dinners which would be cooked in the communal oven and collected at 12 o'clock. My sister Evelyn would usually take our potatoes to the oven on her way to work. One morning she dismounted from her bicycle and took the dish from the carrier. There was only one potato. The others had been lost on the way as she bumped along. She hastily retraced her journey but did not find one. They had all been picked up.

Bill was sorry one lunch hour when he saw a man who was riding his bicycle with a jar of bean soup tied in a cloth hanging from the handlebars. He was on his way home from the furze oven when suddenly the cloth undid and the jar smashed on the road.

The man wept, "That was my family's dinner and we've got nothing else."

I was asked to join a newly formed soup kitchen committee. An empty cottage was put at our disposal. We hired a cook and the committee took turns as helpers. Soup was served once a day. This was particularly popular with men whose wives had evacuated and therefore had to concoct their own meals.

Bill visited one such man in hospital. He was suffering from malnutrition, had drunk pint after pint of water and was swollen to grotesque proportions. Another poor man in the same ward was six feet tall and weighed only six stone.

I developed a hacking and persistent cough. There were no drugs for minor ailments like coughs so finally Bill purchased some black market brandy and poured me a neat dose. He then poured one for himself.

"Just as a precaution," he said.

I gasped as I swallowed the burning liquid. I had eaten little and was unaccustomed to alcohol, I began to giggle and then broke into unrestrained laughter. I laughed until Bill also joined in the hilarity. Whether I was cured by the brandy or the laughter my coughing ceased.

There was one very unpleasant and debilitating ailment from which we nearly all suffered at one time or another and that was dysentery. There was no medicine so we just had to put up with it until it stopped.

We had an old-fashioned copper boiler in our wash house. Bill decided to use it to make sugar beet treacle. He boiled the beetroots, scooped them out of the water and mashed them to pulp with a heavy jack fixed on a frame which stood on a tray into which the juice dripped. The juice was then boiled down until it was the right consistency, then poured into jam jars and allowed to set. Some people added caragen moss to help it to set but Bill never did. Ours was pure sugar beet and very tasty. Everyone was eager to augment their meagre rations so there was always a demand for the treacle. If a children's party was planned treacle would be ordered well in advance and we made sure to keep treacle for these occasions.

Many households used a haybox for cooking. My husband found a wooden box which he filled with dried hay. He then put a saucepan into the box and pressed the hay firmly around it so that when the saucepan was removed its imprint remained.

I would prepare soup, beans or other vegetables in the saucepan, boil them for about five minutes over a fire then quickly put the saucepan into the haybox, cover it over with more hay and place a lid on the box. After a few hours the contents would be beautifully cooked.

The haybox was the equivalent of a very slow oven.

The Old Marais. The authoress's home during the occupation.
Photographed by Bill Gillingham

Chapter 17

GATHERING WOOD

As there was no other fuel we had to burn wood and a mixture of sawdust and tar which made a good fire. We also used this mixture to cook our sugar beet. Due to a shortage of wood we became involved in a risky enterprise.

There was a barbed wire enclosure near La Greve on L'Ancresse Common in which there were piles of wood. At the site there was a wooden hut where the Germans would congregate.

Bill approached Alf Martel who, as I have mentioned before, was completely undaunted by the Germans and had already served two prison sentences for breaking German regulations. He was always finding some way of irritating the enemy.

Bill asked for his help in procuring some German wood from within the barbed wire enclosure. Armed with a large handcart they bribed the local guard to let them in. They could hear the Germans talking and laughing in their hut as they hastily filled the cart with wood.

After a while Bill said uneasily, "That's enough. Let's go." The guard was also worried and had already warned that the soldiers would soon emerge from the hut. Alf was adamant.

"We're here to fill this cart and that's what we're going to do."

They carried on until the cart was groaning under the load before they pushed it out into the road and the welcome darkness of the night.

Forced labour had constructed a railway line across L'Ancresse Common for the train to carry cement and the building materials to build the walls and the large bunkers. Every evening, Alf would saunter across the common and steal the end sleeper of the railway line. He showed Bill a heap of sleepers hidden in his garden.

One night as he strolled along the grass intent on adding to his collection, he was challenged by the guard who took him to the German officer in one of the big bunkers.

In reply to the officer's query, "What were you doing?" Alf explained innocently that one of his cows had been staked on the common and the stake was missing. Alf had been searching for it.

"In future," said the officer, "you will look for your lost property during the day. Do not let us catch you on the common at night".

Alf was dismissed.

German Light Railway which supplied our sleepers!

Chapter 18

PLIGHT OF FOREIGN LABOURERS

One day, Bill found some old chicken feed in a shed at the Hougue Père and asked mother if he could have it. He brought it home, sifted out the husks and suggested that I make pancakes. I had greased the pan with a minimum of fat and had cooked a couple of pancakes when two Dutch boys from the forced labour camp knocked at the door and pleaded, "'ungry, 'ungry."

Bill said generously, "Give them a pancake each and if it doesn't kill them we'll eat the rest!" The boys ate the pancakes as though they were from a Cordon Bleu menu. We ate the rest for tea. They were good, the only drawback being the little husks which stuck in our throats as we swallowed. In spite of this we continued using the mash until there was no more.

We invited the Dutch boys, Heink Vidam and Piet Veen, to come for a meal the following Wednesday and then every Wednesday after that. We were short of food but their plight was far worse than ours. Bill invited them for 6 p.m. but at 5.30 we could see them walking up and down the road. I would cook potatoes when available or make parsnip cake or carrot pudding. Sometimes there were only beans. Afterwards the Dutch boys would stay and play whist. We could not speak each other's languages but it was amazing how well we understood each other. One night as we played I could not take my eyes off Heink's wrist. There was a flea creeping under under his cuff and then coming out again. Today fleas are not the subject of polite conversation but during the occupation you just could not ignore them. They were a fact of life.

Bill always claimed he was so sensitive to fleas that he could tell if one of them had a limp! Each morning when I made the bed there was no such thing as hurrying and covering it over quickly. Every day the bed was stripped and I would search every inch of blanket before covering it over. I had never caught a flea in my life before 1940 but with practice I became very proficient.

Heink Vidam and Piet Veen said that they had been picked up in Holland by a German lorry and told that they were being taken to do half a day's work further on, instead of which they were driven to a Channel Port and shipped to Guernsey with no luggage and dressed in the summer clothes they were wearing.

One Wednesday night, these two Dutch boys arrived looking particularly grim. They told us that they and their workmates stationed at L'Ancresse Lodge Hotel had rebelled against the shocking conditions under which they had to live and work and they had now refused to work. Later that evening there was a knock on our door and two older foreign workers arrived asking to speak to Heink and Piet. They came inside and there ensured a long argument between the four men in rapid Dutch which we could not understand. Eventually the older men left and the others explained the situation.

The Germans had given an ultimatum.

"Either you return to work as usual or every day one man will be shot." Heink said, "Let them shoot." The older men pointed out that they, the old ones, would surely be the first victims and they did not want to die. After these years of misery they clung to the hope that the war would end one day and they would return to their wives and country. There was really no choice, they had to yield.

Foreign labourers were brought to Guernsey to build extensive fortifications, an underground hospital, underground living accommodation, concrete walls, gun emplacements and towers. They had a terrible time and suffered from hunger, cold and ill treatment.

I have referred to a lonely house set in a quiet area in the north of the island. It has the most inappropriate name of 'Paradis'. The Germans used it as a punishment prison for foreign workers who misbehaved and rumours were rife concerning atrocities enacted there.

CANADIAN LEGION
WAR SERVICES Inc.

CANADIAN Y.M.C.A.
OVERSEAS

ON ACTIVE SERVICE

CANADIAN
KNIGHTS OF COLUMBUS
WAR SERVICES

THE SALVATION ARMY
CANADIAN
WAR SERVICES

Amsterdam.
15-1-46.

Dear Mr. and Mrs. Mahy,

Perhaps you'll think it very strange to get this letter, and you'll have to think hard to know from whom it comes. But I'll help you. I've been at your house in the end of '42. I always came there along with my friend Peter, to have dinner. You've got a picture of my wife, that she send. Do you remember how..

I wanted to know how all of you were. I hope that you'll been all right, all during the war. My wife and me are fine. We only had one hard blow. On the day of the liberation my brother in law was shot by the Jerries. It happened on the 5th of may.

4/71 CFA 170   **PLEASE WRITE ON BOTH SIDES**

Copy of a letter sent after the war by one of the Dutch boys,
Piet Veen, to Mr & Mrs Mahy.

I myself, was sent from France to Germany. I've been away from home for over two years. That sure was a horrible long time, but we always were sure though that we would be going home. and at last that day came on the 25th of May.

My wife is often talking about you, although she doesn't know you personally. Now already she's saying that she would like so much that financial part might enable us that we could afford a trip to Guernsey. If she knew already for sure that it would happen would she ever try to learn English.

Well dear people, I hope that this letter will reach you, and that you'll be able to spare a couple of minutes to write to me.

Many greetings from my wife and your always grateful friend.

Piet Veen.

There was a family who had befriended a Dutchman. He arrived one evening and said that he had been imprisoned for some time at Paradis for stealing carrots.

"So you're fee again," remarked his friends.

"No, I'm only free for a few hours and I'm ashamed to tell you the reason."

The family persuaded him to tell them. He admitted that his gaoler had ordered him to go out and steal a hen or rabbit from a Guernsey family with the promise of a dire penalty if he returned empty handed.

Edwin Creber lived with his parents in the vicinity of Paradis and was very aware of the inhuman treatment meted out to the unhappy inmates. In the spring of 1943 his mother remarked that she had seen what appeared to be a load of furniture being unloaded in Paradis garden.

The sea wall at L'Ancresse built by forced labour imported by the Germans. (Photograph by Bill Gillingham)

"Probably commandeered from some unfortunate Guernsey family," she added.

Later that evening Edwin and his brother set out to investigate. They soon discovered that this mysterious load of furniture was in fact a load of coffins dumped under the front windows in full view of the occupants of the house.

There was talk that the Germans buried some of their victims from Paradis on a tip which was situated fairly near to my father's vinery. One day, when nobody was around, he and one of his men went to investigate and they found a rough coffin with the completely naked emaciated body of an unfortunate lad. He knew then that the rumours were true.

Indeed one night, just before Liberation in 1945, Bill was standing with my father not far from the tip near Les Petils beach when a lorry passed close to them. They could see that in it there were soldiers wearing masks. These soldiers had a grim task to perform. The Germans knew that the end of the war was imminent and the bodies buried on the tip must not be found by the British. They had to be dug out and reburied.

Chapter 19

HARD TIMES

One Sunday as he was walking to church Bill's father saw two foreign workers scraping for potatoes in a field. Two Germans noticed them and shouted at them. The men ran and the soldiers ordered them to halt. One man stopped, the other ran on and the soldier raised his gun and shot him.

Another foreign labourer was more fortunate when he questioned German authority. Rudolf was a tall strong Dutch lad and one morning when he reported for work, the German in charge of the work party accused him of being absent the previous day. Rudolf angrily denied the charge and struck the German. He was promptly marched to the commanding officer, there was a trial and it was proved that Rudolf was right and it was another man who had been absent. Rudolf and the German soldier were both punished.

The officer declared, "Nobody strikes a German." Turning to the soldier he added, "A German never makes a mistake."

First Rudolf was made to crawl over a stony patch on his hands and knees until he reached a certain tree where a soldier waited clutching a piece of hosepipe. Rudolf then had to climb the tree until he reached the branch indicated and, as he climbed, the German hit him continuously with the hosepipe. He was, however, considerably cheered when the German underwent the same punishment.

Rudolf reported gleefully, "I was taller than him and so he took longer to reach the branch!"

At 7 a.m. one morning in the early summer of 1943 Rosa Simonet, who lived in Burnt Lane, St Peter Port, was disturbed by loud angry shouts. Her bedroom commanded an excellent view to the West and the surrounding area. She looked out of the bay window towards the commotion.

The houses along Vauvert were occupied by foreign workers and halfway up the hill stood a furious German soldier shouting and waving his arms threateningly. Two of the foreign labourers emerged and spoke to him then Rosa saw them disappear inside the house. A moment later she saw a man hurtle through the top window to the pavement below. The two men rushed through the door and picked up the motionless body and, followed by the German soldier, they started walking up the hill towards the foreign workers' hospital near Vauvert School. Rosa did not know if the man had been pushed or if he had jumped out in fear of the enemy.

We were told that one slave labourer, driven to desperation by the German in charge, raised his long razor sharp spade and, in a fury, dealt the German such a blow that his head was completely severed. The man was immediately shot.

Nicholas Mahy and his wife Elise were good, kind Guernsey people who lived at Sandy Hook with their eighteen year old daughter, Bertha. Nicholas was walking by the German Railway at L'Islet when he met one of the foreign labourers. This man Lucien, an Algerian in his late thirties, said that he was faced with a desperate problem. He was due to leave the island the following day but did not want to go. He was afraid of the change and terrified of where he might be taken. He pleaded with Nicholas.

"All I need is shelter for two days. I have a friend who is eager to get away and willing to change identity cards with me and I could stay in his place."

Nicholas took Lucien home and he and his wife Elise agreed to hide Lucien for two days. Nicholas admitted later that this was the biggest mistake of their lives. The two days extended to weeks, months, years. Nicholas and his wife had committed an offence in harbouring Lucien in the first place and were in danger of being deported if they were caught.

The Algerian had no ration book so the family was obliged to share their meagre rations. He could not help Nicholas by working in the greenhouses because he could not risk being seen. Lucien became moody and bad tempered. He could be heard pacing the bedroom muttering to himself. Nicholas' friends knew that there was an Algerian living there, but were not aware of the true circumstances. They assumed he was working as a forced labourer.

When Bertha went out with her friends in the evening, she was always glad when she was escorted home by one of the boys from among her group of friends. She was nervous about meeting Lucien in the lonely lane leading to her house. When he was restlessly walking around in the night, she slept in her parents' room.

One day, Bertha and her mother were alone in the cellar scrubbing beetroots prior to making sugar beet syrup. Two German officers strode in and accused Elise of harbouring a missing Algerian worker.

Elise replied indignantly, "Certainly not. How do you think we could manage to feed another man when we can just about keep ourselves from starving?"

The Germans continued their questioning but Elise remained adamant. She was fully aware that she, her husband and daughter were in grave danger and she remained outwardly calm and convincing although inwardly shaking with terror.

When the officers had gone Elise and Bertha went up to the house but could not find Lucien. He was hiding in a wardrobe.

He returned to France after the war. The family received a latter from him to which they did not reply. They felt they had suffered enough and wanted no more of him.

Chapter 20

ONE FAMILY'S STORY

Edward Rowe lived in a large house at the Friquet in the Castel Parish and it was not long before it was requisitioned by the enemy. Mr. & Mrs. Rowe took up residence at 'Brookfield' nearby, the home of their son George.

Edward was a fern specialist and when he was told to clear his fern and grow food for the Germans he flatly refused. He remained adamant and after the enemy had commandeered his yacht, which was never seen again, he and his wife were sent to France with a group of English born people. On reaching France the men and women were separated. The men went to Biberach Internment Camp. Six months elapsed before the women were taken there as well. So Edward and his wife Mary were both at Biberach living in separate quarters and there they remained until the end of the war.

It was not long before George Rowe's home was invaded by eight or nine soldiers. The house was big so George and his wife Muriel with their two children remained at 'Brookfield' in a flat upstairs.

They remember one German who was a comical sight at night. He wore an ankle length night-shirt and with his steel rimmed spectacles he resembled an absent-minded professor carrying a rifle.

The soldiers always carried their rifles and George was amused that, despite the enemy's usually excessive precautions, one particular soldier would always place his rifle outside the lavatory door. He could have been shot with his own gun as he emerged.

There was a constant German guard on the house and it was very disconcerting when the family was in bed at night to have a torch flashed in their faces as their identity was checked.

Eventually George and Muriel had to leave their home to the

enemy. They moved to Sohier House in the Vale Parish. Here George had a workshop where he made small wireless sets known as crystal sets. By this time the wireless sets in the island had been confiscated, though there were a few people who kept a set hidden somewhere on their premises.

A crystal set. These were made locally in large numbers.

George's crystal sets were very popular. We bought one and so did many other families. We still have ours. It lived in a rabbit box in the shed during the war. At first George experimented with bottles of salt water to replace batteries and then he made crystals with lead and sulphur. A pair of headphones was needed and we received the Forces' programmes loud and clear, but not the BBC Home Service.

There was always a feeling of insecurity when George was busy manufacturing his crystal sets. He had to be prepared for a German to walk in unannounced at any time. On one occasion this happened when a German came into the house to ask the way. He then began taking an interest in the contents of the workshop. Gerald Sparkes, who was there at the time, drew the German's attention to a bicycle which was being repaired while George worked on at his bench hiding away any incriminating evidence.

Towards the end of the war George remembers seeing a line of German soldiers systematically poking into the ground of the field opposite. They were looking for pieces of vegetables left in the soil, so great was their hunger. He recollects seeing a young German shaking and weeping and when asked what was wrong the soldier replied that he had just heard that his home town had been heavily bombed.

Muriel's parents were English born and so deported from Jersey to Wurzach Internment Camp. Their unmarried daughter Nancy had just recovered from rheumatic fever and her parents said she was not fit to travel.

The officer looked at Nancy and replied, "You can stand on your feet, you go."

When at Wurzach sometimes they would go for walks under supervision and in crocodile formation and remembered the kindness of some of the local people. Red Cross parcels were received in camp. They remembered a group of prisoners who were brought to their camp one night and then moved on next morning. Nobody was able to speak with the newcomers and the camp dwellers deduced that they must be either Jews or political prisoners. They looked a terrible sight, people with all hope gone, pale, worn, emaciated. Where would their journey end?

Chapter 21

WIRELESS SETS

Once wireless sets were finally confiscated there were severe penalties for being found in possession of a set.

One day I was in the dining room on the left of the front door and Bill was in the kitchen directly opposite the front door. A German strode in without knocking. Bill knew that I was listening to the news on the crystal set, so he went towards the soldier.

"Cigarette?" he said, offering one of his home-made efforts. By this time I was stuffing the set in a cupboard. The soldier never glanced my way. He took the cigarette, asked for directions and went out through the back door.

A Guernseyman was sitting by his fire listening to the news when he heard a German burst into the house. A saucepan was bubbling on the grate and on hearing the commotion the man hastily plunged his set into the soup. The German policeman entered the room and declared,

"We have been informed that you have a wireless set. Where is it?"

"You have been misinformed," replied the man mildly, "but you are welcome to search if you like."

The German stared at him and demanded in his loud guttural voice, "if you have no set, why are you wearing earphones?"

The Hoolahans who lived at Delancey had their wireless set hidden under the floorboards in a bedroom. They were listening to a programme when there was a disturbance outside. There were Germans in the road. Jack Hoolahan hurriedly covered the gap in the floor with the linoleum without replacing the floorboards.

Later, the local priest, Father Kirk, came to hear the news.

He strode into the room and fell straight down the hole, through the linoleum on to the set.

During one of the first months of the occupation a neighbour asked if he could store his pram in our shed as he had no room in his.

We readily agreed. After the war he fetched his pram and asked if we had ever looked inside it.

Bill replied "Certainly not, it just remained there as you had left it." The man laughed and showed us that underneath the covers was a new wireless set which he had not wanted to part with when the island sets were collected. We were furious. If our shed had been searched and the set found, nobody would have believed that we knew nothing about it.

Wireless set and camera confiscation receipts.

Chapter 22

LOCAL ENTERPRISE

Bill planted tobacco plants in a greenhouse. When they were ready he picked the large green leaves and between us we passed them through an old fashioned mangle until they were well and truly squashed, after which Bill hung them on the greenhouse cross wires to dry. When satisfied that they were crisp and dry he took a parcel of them to Bucktrout to be crushed and rolled into cigarettes. They looked perfect, better than they tasted! However the men still smoked them and if they happened to cough or breathe heavily while smoking, burning ash spluttered everywhere. We called it the 'scorched earth policy' when we saw the little holes on chairs and carpets.

Salt, or lack of it, was another problem. We tried cooking vegetables in a mixture of sea water and fresh water. Later, Bill had some long shallow tin trays constructed which we laid on top of the beams in the greenhouse. We took a handcart laden with buckets and other containers and went to the beach to fill them with sea-water. Back we trudged to the vinery. Bill climbed the steps and tipped the buckets of salt water into the tins. After some time the water had evaporated leaving a crust of salt in the pans. We collected the salt into jars and refilled the tins so there was always plenty of salt.

Until we were forbidden access to the beaches, we learned to distinguished carrageen moss from the other seaweed. We collected , dried, and used it as jelly. It looked more appetising when we added a few drops of cochineal to give it colour.

Fishermen had a petrol allowance to go fishing. Naturally there were German patrol boats around. There was always a long queue at the fish shops waiting for the fishermen's return. A certain percentage of the fish had to be kept for the Germans and we queued for the remainder with our ration books.

One day on a very low tide, Bill took his basket and went to L'Ancresse beach to look for ormers. Other men were already there busily turning the rocks over and filling their baskets with this precious food. When they reached the top of the beach, soaking wet but with food for the family, they were lined up by an angry German corporal who was strutting around importantly demanding to see everybody's identity cards.

The corporal began at one end examining the cards, shouting threats at each one. How dare they take anything off the beach without permission? They were not allowed to be there anyway and, scarlet in the face, he ranted on. There were more than a dozen men and one of them, Charlie Le Lievre, was a member of our local police. There was going to be real trouble for him when it was his turn to show his identity card.

When the German was examining Jack Sebire's card and making accusations, Jack protested that he did not know that he was breaking the law. With his face an inch from Jack's nose, the German told him exactly what would happen if he transgressed again. He was so excited that he did not notice Charlie Le Lievre quietly slip over from the end of the line that had not yet been checked to the other end which had, thus never having to produce his card.

Another time Bill went to L'Eree. There he started ormering, ready with the excuse that he did not know it was not allowed in case he was challenged. On his return an officer was waiting with his rifle.

"Do you realise," he said, "that you have been in a forbidden area under our guns and that I would have been in my rights to shoot you?"

He continued lecturing in this vein, but to Bill's immense relief he did not confiscate his catch and let him go with a warning.

In the late autumn, after the wheat and corn had been cut and harvested we would mount our bicycles and with a sack on our backs we would pedal to the upper parishes where the farms were more numerous than in the Vale.

We chose a field in St Saviours and, starting at one end, began to glean the scattered heads of wheat. Other people were doing likewise so we continued gleaning until the fields were clean and we could find no more wheat.

When the wheat was dried we ground it into flour through a coffee grinder. It was tedious work but the flour was a welcome addition to our meagre rations.

As time passed and our bicycle tyres could no longer be mended we used hosepipe for tyres. As I have already stated cycling was very strenuous especially against the wind! In 1940 all cars had been requisitioned so old and young were riding cycles.

Once Bill and I were caught and fined by the Germans for riding our bicycles two abreast, this dreadful crime was subsequently reported in the local Press!

When I look back I wish that I had the forethought shown by my aunt, Mrs Elise Le Masurier, a Jersey farmer's wife.

During 1939, before rationing began my aunt made plans to deal with food shortages. She remembered the hardships of the First World War and thus was better prepared than many. She made bread, baked it, then proceeded to slice and toast it. Her husband purchased fifteen new potato barrels which Elise patiently lined up and filled one by one with the toasted slices which were carefully wrapped and sealed.

This was a long and tedious task. The bread did not become mouldy because the moisture had been toasted away. her daughter still remembers the bread puddings they ate during the occupation.

Bill was Communion Steward at our church throughout the war. This meant that he prepared the bread and wine. The wine was symbolic, just coloured water, but the bread was real. The baker supplied a free loaf for the Communion and we cut it into small squares, small being the operative word, because what remained of the loaf belonged to us. There was a complaint that the portions were too small!

The small chunk of hard soap which was our ration was both woefully inadequate and impossible to lather. During 1941 I placed an advert in the 'Press' offering to exchange tea for soap. I still have the written replies.

The one which I accepted reads as follows:-

"Dear Madam,

Re. advert. I can exchange 4 bars of Puritan olive oil soap (3½lbs) for ½lb Lyons tea.

Yours truly,

C. de G.B."

Barter shop in the Arcade, St Peter Port. (Secretly photographed.)

Chapter 23

LIFE LINE

Our crystal set was unable to receive the BBC Home Service so when we knew that Churchill was going to broadcast Bill would go to Cliff Farnham's home, seven or eight minutes away at the Jamblin, to listen to the big wireless set which Cliff kept in the shed. The Forces' News was preceded by the opening bars of Beethoven's 5th Symphony and many years later it gives me a strange feeling to hear that particular music.

One night, Churchill was going to make a speech so Bill and John Bailey went, after curfew, to hear the Prime Minister on Cliff's set. The speech, in Churchill's inimitable style, warmed their hearts and spirits. After listening to the broadcast they set off quietly into the dark night. John Bailey was carrying a stout stick.

Bill enquired what the stick was for but john just nodded nervously and said, "You never know." Suddenly they heard heavy footsteps coming towards them through the inky blackness of the night.

"Come on," Bill said, "over the wall and across the fields." John remained, stick in hand, immobile in the middle of the road. The steps were coming nearer.

"Come on, John." Bill urged from over the wall, but John just could not move. He stood there, petrified. Bill made his way home and waited in the garden to find out what had happened.

Soon afterwards, John Bailey came along and explained that it had been impossible for him to move, he just waited there and suddenly the steps had quickened into a run and next thing he knew a body collided heavily into him.

It was Tom Le Page who had been listening to Churchill on his own set and had decided to run out quickly and tell his friend the news. He put his head on his arms against the wall and laughed and laughed. He could not stop. John had a shock but he had heard the footsteps approaching unlike poor Tom. Tom's wife said afterwards that he had laughed hysterically all night.

Listening to the wireless was not always a pleasurable experience. Sometimes when we were 'listening in' the well-known and much hated voice of James Joyce, known as 'Lord Haw Haw', would intrude upon the programme with his fake propaganda. Even though we knew he was an English traitor it was depressing to hear him describe enemy successes at great length and listing the Allies' losses.

One clear starlit night we were awakened by loud shouts and the sound of running footsteps along the road. We opened our window and looked out. Several German soldiers were running along with sacks on their backs.

The reason they were running in fright was because Tom Le Page had heard them while they were stealing his rabbits and he was shouting after them. Everywhere windows were opening and people joining in the shouting.

Clare Tupper from 'Le Hautgard' called across the night, "What's happening?"

I replied, "It's the German army in full retreat." We all laughed.

The soldiers were terrified because if they had been caught by their superiors they would have been in trouble. They could have been sent to Russia, which was there greatest dread.

Chapter 24

ALL NIGHT PARTIES

I particularly remember one all-night party at our home. We invited Bert Perchard to bring his film projector and films from Alderney. We played cards and Christmas games, then we had a film show. My favourite film was one in which George Formby sang 'When I'm cleaning windows.'

Bert also daringly showed a film of the British Navy coming out of the dock while the band played 'Land of Hope and Glory.' The music shook the house! We were in festive mood but it was a good thing that the German patrol did not pass at that moment.

We had prepared beds upstairs for the girls. We fell into them at about 4 a.m. and the men slept on the floor downstairs. Some stayed up and played the card game 'euchre'.

At another party, this time held at Tom and Rose Henry's home at 'Eastbourne', we decided that we would stay up all night. At one point we all sat around the table with the tips of our fingers touching and asked the table questions. The table would knock the floor in reply and everyone vowed that nobody had moved it.

"How many children does Henry have?"

The table promptly knocked twice. We were delighted with our success until Bill, always the sceptic, asked Rose if she knew how many stairs there were to her top landing. Neither she nor Tom had ever counted.

"Right," Bill asked the table, "how many stairs are there to the top landing of this house?"

The table obediently tapped away and eventually stopped. We all rushed out to count the stairs. The table was wrong.

"There you are," Bill declared triumphantly. "I said someone was pushing!"

When planning the party, Tom and Rose had asked everybody to contribute some item of entertainment. Anyone too shy to perform could play a favourite record. There followed a most entertaining hour. Bill's songs were always in great demand. He sang Arthur Askey's 'Moth Song' complete with actions, and I recited a poem which Bill composed.

There Is An Occupation

There's an occupation that means when armies come,
There's an occupation – invasion by the Hun,
In mass evacuation mothers and children go,
Away from homes and loved ones, fleeing from the foe.

There's an occupation that brings you down a peg,
When you've ripped your trousers and you've got to paint your leg.
There's an occupation when it's hard to feed a mouse,
The only mice that are well fed are up at Hirzel House.

There's an occupation when it's bad for girls and boys,
It means when Father Christmas comes he can't bring any toys.
There's an occupation that finds you at your best,
When this occupation goes it leaves you in your vest.

There's an occupation when you wake up in the night,
And 'round your bed there's wandering a stranger with a light.
There's an occupation when for tyres we have hose,
When the little wire breaks, you end up on your nose.

There's an occupation when we haven't any fats,
We haven't any kittens and we haven't any cats.
At first there came the order, all dogs must be tied,
And now upon his menu, Jerry has them boiled or fried.

There's an occupation when we've treasures just a few,

We hide them underneath the bed or stick them up the flue,
Our bicycles and hens, inside the house and shed we park,
Our goats and rabbits follow in a modern Noah's Ark.

There's an occupation that has left us empty chairs,
There's an occupation that has caused us anxious fears.
There'll be an occupation when these chairs we'll fill once more,
When will this occupation be? In 1944.

By Wilson Mahy, 1943

The following Christmas, 1944, I was requested to repeat the poem.
I did with a slight alteration to the last two lines.

'There'll be an occupation when to fill these chairs we'll strive,
When will that occupation be? In 1945.'

And it was.

Setting off for Rosemary Henry's christening 1943.
Godmother, Eileen Collas (holding baby) with
Tom and Rose Henry outside 'Eastbourne'.

Chapter 25

HUNGER

Bill and John Pattimore decided to go into business together in their spare time making cigarette paper books. They cut the paper into strips and gummed one edge, then bound them together into small booklets.

The first batch was unsuccessful and was burnt. The next attempt was a great improvement and the books sold well. The trouble was that after a time the home grown tobacco ran out, therefore there was no demand for cigarette papers and the business closed.

One day when John and Bill were busy with the paper strips in the shed, a German soldier walked in and asked for food.

He was told that there was no food but he lingered and said, "There will be food by and by, the war will soon be over."

At that moment John, who was working upstairs, moved around.

The soldier's face was ashen, he looked terrified. "Who is that?" he stammered.

"Oh," said Bill, "that's my friend, he's working upstairs." Had it been one of the German police, the soldier knew that he would have been shot for anticipating a German defeat.

As the Germans grew hungrier it became clear that Guernsey people's pets were being eaten. Bill's brother had an endearing grey and black spaniel named Patch. He was of a most friendly disposition and everyone loved him. One day he was missing.

Later my Aunt Rachel recollected that on that particular afternoon when she was walking down the lane leading to her home she saw Patch. A German soldier was patting him and Patch was responding in his usual amiable fashion.

Aunt Rachel thought to herself, "I don't like the Germans, but they can't be all bad. I can see how that soldier loves dogs."

Patch was never seen again!

Mrs. Daubert, my neighbour, had a favourite cat which never strayed far from the garden. One morning two Germans called and asked for food. I replied that I had none.

Later that day she asked anxiously if I had seen Timmy, her black and white cat. On reflection I realised I had not seen him since that morning and immediately guessed what had happened.

The following day I recognised the same Germans passing the house.

Furious, I banged on the window, opened it and called accusingly, "You, you katze essen."

"Nein, nein, ich bin katzenkamerad," one soldier replied.

I regretted that my knowledge of the German language was almost non-existent so I could only reiterate until they were out of earshot, "You, katze essen."

Vega bringing the life saving Red Cross parcels and bread to hungry islanders. (Photograph courtesy of Peter and Paul Balshaw)

Rabbits were difficult to rear, there was little suitable food and one day a friend found his finest rabbit lying dead in its hutch. When darkness fell he hung the carcass from a low branch of a tree near the road and, knowing that the Germans were always on the prowl, he declared, I'll wager that it will be gone by morning." It was.

A Guernsey girl was working as housemaid in a house that had been commandeered by the Germans and one of the soldiers invited her to stay for lunch. Having so little food at home, she was sorely tempted and she stayed. She ate heartily the best meal she had had for a long time. A soldier asked her later if she had enjoyed her lunch. She had, but when he informed her that the meat was cat she turned green, flew outside, and was violently sick.

One night we were awakened by a terrible commotion. It was the noise of crashing glass and amid the pandemonium the loud shouts of a man in a frenzy. As we rushed to the window we saw what I can only describe as a mad soldier yelling as he flung stone after stone at the greenhouse just across the road, while the glass come clattering down. It was a horrifying sound.

Bill went downstairs and dialled the Police but could get no reply. Nobody wanted to know. He was careful to remain hidden in case the soldier turned around and aimed at our windows, however the man concentrated on the greenhouses. The smashing noise and the shouts diminished as the German journeyed on, shattering windows as he went. The story heard later was that he was due to go to the Russian front and, overcome with fear, had gone berserk. We never heard what eventually happened to him.

Once a month we ate Sunday lunch at the home of my favourite uncle and aunt, Edwin and Rachel Mahy. One Sunday, it must have been late February or March, we were particularly hungry. Our winter stock of potatoes, our staple diet, had run out and we felt a persistent craving for food. When we sat down to my aunt's baked potatoes and rabbit stew I must admit that we ate ravenously.

Tea time arrived and we had mashed potatoes and beans. We had brought our own two slices of bread to eat with the Carrageen moss jelly. Again we ate with immense enjoyment. During the evening I felt as if the room had begun to swim and I had a strange feeling in my stomach and throat. I rushed outside and was extremely sick.

Bill declared that we must go home immediately since I was not feeling well. He was in a hurry because he did not want my aunt and uncle to know he was also feeling very unwell. We walked the short journey home along a narrow lane and we both had to stop and vomit over the wall several times before reaching home empty and exhausted, but still feeling queasy. Our stomachs just could not take the extra food.

1944 dawned with bleak prospects for the future. The island was terribly short of food and there was no more bread. The situation for the Germans was becoming desperate. They were now like the foreign labourers, eating old cabbage stalks in the fields and anything they could scavenge.

One man tells a story of the soldiers' increasing weakness. Living opposite German lodgings he would watch the Germans enter their garden. When a soldier would use his hands to lift his leg over the step, the man knew that he would not see that soldier many more times.

Comfortably built Guernsey men and women were now thin and scrawny with loose skin, noticeably around the neck and arms. We were hungry all the time but strangely one became accustomed to hunger and could ignore it. We knew that there was no more food therefore we did not look for it or worry about it. We ate our sparse diet and carried on with the business of survival. We discovered how little food one needs to exist.

In the midst of this gloomy winter came the 'Vega', the Red Cross boat filled with bread and Red Cross parcels from Australia and New Zealand. Fifty years later I can still visualise that first Red Cross loaf. We could not believe that bread looked and tasted like that loaf. It was like manna from heaven.

After this we received a ration of bread and, every month, a Red Cross parcel.

My joy was tinged with sadness as I wished that my beloved old aunts, Rachel and Mary, had survived long enough to enjoy the arrival of the Vega. They had settled uncomplainingly to a life of great privation but it had taken its toll. Rachel had died in 1942 and Mary in 1943.

We heard a sad story about one man living alone who received his Red Cross parcel one Thursday morning and by Sunday he had finished it and smoked the tea. On Monday he was dead. The concentrated food was intended to last a month and his shrivelled stomach just could not take it in three days.

Contents of New Zealand Red Cross Parcel
6 oz sugar
19 oz corned mutton
15 oz of lamb and green peas
8 oz chocolate
20 oz butter
15 oz of coffee and milk
9 oz dried peas
16 oz condensed milk
15 oz of cheese
10 oz sugar
16 oz jam
6 oz raisins

Total amount: 135 oz of food.

Contents of Canadian Red Cross Parcel
6 oz chocolate
20 oz biscuits
5 oz sardines
20 oz milk powder
6 oz prunes
20 oz ham
10 oz salmon
14 oz corned beef
8 oz sugar
4 oz cheese
16 oz marmalade
1 cake of soap

Chapter 26

FREEDOM AT LAST

In 1945 we were aware both from the news on our crystal sets and from reports that filtered through the grapevine, that the war was ending at long last.

A local man with a knowledge of German hid behind a hedge to listen to soldiers who were being lectured by an officer.

The officer stated that their armies were sorely pressed but he declared in words to this effect, "We will never surrender the Channel Islands, we will fight to the last man. We stay even if we have to eat grass."

Throughout early May rumour and counter-rumour buzzed over the length and breadth of the island. Would the German Army fulfil its threat and fight for the islands? We were aware of furious activity on the French coast, all night long air traffic droned overhead and clouds of smoke were visible on the horizon.

On the last day of our occupation, Tuesday May 8th 1945, the weather was exactly the same as it had been on the terrible day when the enemy invaded. The air was balmy and quiet, the sun rose with the promise of a gorgeous day.

The previous night had been busy with overhead traffic and Bill set off for work on his bicycle as usual. It was close to midday when a friend came running up to the greenhouse where Bill was raking the paths.

"The war is over! The war is over!" he shouted.

Bill dropped his rake and pedalled for home.

People were talking excitedly together in the roads and calling out the good news as he passed. He entered the 'Maison de Bas' kitchen where our meal was cooking in the communal furze oven.

Mrs Belloeil, a cheerful lady, was in charge of the dinners and as Bill approached he could hear her singing lustily as she worked.

When he entered Bill remarked, "Well, the war is over."

"Never!" She stared at him in disbelief as she handed him his dish. "It's another of your jokes."

"It's not a joke this time, it's true and Churchill is making a speech this afternoon."

The truth slowly dawned and, with her head cradled in her arms on the bench, she sobbed as loudly as she had sung.

There was excitement and elation everywhere.

In the early afternoon we set off to the 'Tertre', where a wireless set had been rescued from its hiding place and brought into the lounge. A group of friends gathered to hear Churchill speak.

When he said, "Our dear Channel Islands will be freed today," several people wept.

The five long years of Nazi occupation were over.

It was overwhelming, almost unbelievable.

The visible proof lay in the fact that lying at anchor outside the harbour were two British Naval ships, HMS Bulldog and HMS Beagle. The following morning, Wednesday May 9th 1945, a force of British soldiers landed on our shores. This was our Liberation Day. Again the weather rejoiced with us. It was a glorious summer day and every able-bodied person headed for town to be part of the general rejoicing.

A small group of us rode our bicycles to St. Sampson's harbour and at William Bowditch's invitation, joined him in his fishing boat.

The following is an account of our expedition as published in the Guernsey Evening Press.

....

"First to welcome the Navy,

Shortly after 9 o'clock on Wednesday morning a party of 13 Northerners left St. Sampson's harbour in Mr. W. Bowditch's boat to go and greet the crew of one of the ships anchored in the roadsteads. Shortly afterwards they were alongside HMS Bulldog and were given a great reception by the crew, comprising British, Belgian and French sailors.

The crew loaded the party with presents of chocolate, tobacco and cigarettes and sweets, which were shared with fellow islanders on the party's return to shore.

In return, the crew received reichsmarks and pfenning pieces as souvenirs. As the demand exceeded the supply, the party put in at St. Peter Port harbour and one of them, Mr. E. D. Collas, called at the Westminster Bank where the clerks made a collection among themselves and these souvenirs were distributed among the sailors on the return trip.

The party also carried copies of the souvenir edition of the 'Evening Press' and back numbers of the German newspaper the 'Deutsche Guernsey Zeitung' which were eagerly accepted by the crew, who informed the Guernsey party that they had spent last Christmas in Russia.

This time the party boarded the ship and exchanged addresses, photographs and autographs. The crew were highly amused when told of the scarcity of cats on the island and as a compensation exhibited their mascot, a huge cat. The sight of a German receipt for a fine imposed on Mr. & Mrs. Wilson Mahy for cycling abreast caused great laughter among the sailors.

As the small boat drew away from the naval vessel, William Bowditch called for three cheers for the crew and the sailors reciprocated with rousing cheers for the Channel Islanders. "It warmed our hearts," was how Mr. Wilson Mahy described it."

Guernsey Evening Press, Thursday May 10, 1945

When we had climbed the ladder and were on the deck of HMS Bulldog chatting with the soldiers an officer came with orders from the bridge. We must leave the ship, we were not permitted aboard because the Bailiff and the Guernsey reception party had not yet arrived. That was the reason for the newspaper headline. Our small group was literally the first to welcome the Navy.

Our little boat with its delighted passengers went back to its mooring in St. Sampson's harbour and we all dispersed to our various homes. We had something to eat, then we climbed on our bicycles again heading for St. Peter Port eager to be in the midst of what was going on.

We sat on the wall opposite the Royal Hotel and watched the crowd milling to and fro, hugging the smiling soldiers as they passed. It was strange to see a relatively small force of British soldiers compared with the thousands of Germans on the island, yet now that the tables were turned the power was with the few.

"I have never had such an experience as this in all my life, and I feel like crying." These were the words spoken to a reporter by Colonel Power, leader of the liberation troops.

He was witness to a tumultuous welcome given to the British soldiers, to the happiness and joyous excitement pervading the island, to the release of pent-up emotions of prisoners set free after five long years of Nazi domination.

This was what we had waited for, deliverance and freedom. We were free - at last.

*Liberation at last! Colin Stoneman being hugged by an islander
outside the Royal Court House on May 12th 1945.*

ACKNOWLEDGEMENTS

Bill Gillingham A.R.P.S., A.F.I.A.R. for taking the cover photograph and those of The Old Marais and L'Ancresse Wall.
Fiona Adams for the photograph of the authoress.

Other photographs by kind permission of:
Richard Heaume (German Occupation Museum)
The Guernsey Press Co. Ltd.
Victor Coysh and Carel Toms
Peter and Paul Bradshaw
R K Mahy
Bill Gillingham
Rosemary Henry.

My thanks to Jane, Carol and Sarah for their interest and support throughout, and in the case of the 2007 revised edition, to Richard Heaume and to Jane for their advice and help.

Miriam Mahy, the authoress, aged 93 in 2007.